Level Up
Your Time with
God

Patrick DA Sims

ISBN 978-1-09808-396-0 (paperback)
ISBN 978-1-09808-397-7 (digital)

Christian Faith Publishing, Inc.
832 Park Avenue
Meadville, PA 16335
www.christianfaithpublishing.com

Printed in the United States of America

Dedicated to my amazing wife, Amy, for not just dealing with but encouraging, my video games. My daughter, Sarah, who is four but already enjoys games. The video game designers who make amazing stories, most of whom don't realize how much, with their creations, they are emulating their own Creator.

Contents

Introduction

There has long been a perceived gap between video games and anything to do with Jesus that isn't a horribly cheesy Bible game. I have played video games since I was little, and I didn't grow up knowing Jesus. I had grown up learning that I had to do good works to make God happy, and a lot of the things in video games felt like they were less than helpful, but since it felt so hard to make God happy, I decided to just have fun and play any game I could either talk my parents into letting me play or play at a friend's house.

Then I heard how Jesus died on the cross, which I knew, but that he didn't just die and rise again, rather that he did it to freely forgive my sins. That radically changed my life and my heart and my mind.

It wasn't an instant change, and I did a lot of things I'd say I learned from doing it wrong the first several times. I even pulled something out of The Stanley Parable and tried to see how many times I could get away with ignoring the "narrator" (God) in my life and still not get in too much trouble. But God stuck by me, forgave me, and helped me learn despite myself.

Things haven't been easy. I've seen my younger brother die, lost all my grandparents, and a beloved father-in-law passed away while I was overseas, had a kid, and had so many incredible experiences, stresses, and dangers that it'd be a whole separate book.

I've been led by God all around the world, got married, been a missionary to Thailand teaching English in the huge city of Bangkok, then teaching a tiny town called Manorom, in a small province called Chai Nat, and teaching at a technical college in Uthai Thani. I've seen God move in huge ways and in little ways. I've been blessed with helping lead people to Christ in three continents. All while I never cut video games out of my life. And while I've learned some things about some games I needed to not play, video games have helped me learn from God, learn about God, and teach about God to others. I've taught history at a small Christian school, and I've never made much money, but I've always seen God provide in the most unusual and usual ways, including him providing enough money for video games.

But also, many well-meaning people have given me strange looks when they find out how much I play video games and that I love Jesus so much as well.

That's where this book's concept came from, wanting to show people how the two are not only reconcilable, but we can "Level Up Your Time with God" by finding God in our video games. Some chapters are even just me remembering conversations I've had with people who either loved video games and Jesus or weren't sure how video games and Jesus could fit together.

Take the time to apply each chapter in this book to your life before, or while moving onto the next chapter, and really approach this with an attitude of getting the most out of it. Like a loading screen that tells you the tips we need before getting completely pwned by whatever is coming after that loading screen, pay attention and don't take it for granted. It's much nicer to win on the first time around rather than have to come back after twenty or thirty game overs.

There are questions to help you process what you're learning as well as help you think through things to reinforce them in your memory, and even if you don't feel like writing the answers down, take the time to answer them and feel free to ask modified versions to others.

Don't skip the last chapter just because it's marked "end credits," there's a lot in there for you as far as resources and ideas as well as some of my favorite video games I've played.

Watch out for the achievements at the end of each chapter. While they don't give you gamer points, they are helpful in seeing the value in what you just learned (and let's face it, achievements are just plain fun to have).

Just to get this out of the way at the beginning, and I'll repeat it at the end: make sure you look at a game's ratings and reason for said ratings before playing it just because it is in this book. I used references from games across genres and rating systems, but not all of them are ones I would recommend personally or for everyone.

I hope and pray this book helps you and that you find God in your video games because he is always worth finding!

With love, in Christ,
Patrick DA Sims

CHAPTER 1

Don't Be a N00b

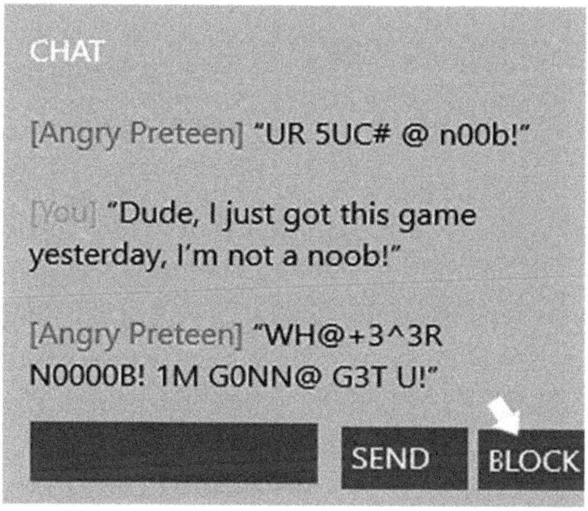

This type of interaction may have very well happened to you, and there's nothing quite like getting falsely called a noob, especially when you're just new to the game. But the big question that every gamer has to ask themselves sometimes is, "Have I become a n00b?"

When we begin to yell irrationally, throw controllers, type with numbers to hide the words we don't want blocked, think we're the expert to end all at a game without ever winning any kind of tournament or holding any records or trying to hack online games to get new gear are just some of the warning signs we're going the wrong way.

In the same way, sometimes we got saved a long time ago, maybe too long to even remember much about it. That salvation felt real at the time, but the desire for anything spiritual has slowly been replaced by internet, video games, computers, social media, and a slew of other things that give us no desire for church, the Bible, God, or anything else in that realm to the point where it feels like listening a cutscene of a fighting game with a boring narrator saying a list of all Pokémon ever made in alphabetical order. That salvation got to the point that it leaves us wondering if it ever happened in the first place.

Important note: *THIS* book is definitely NOT about getting rid of our video games or social media or computers.

It's about seeing the real issues beyond them. And it all starts here with deciding one important thing: Are you a spiritual n00b, a newb, or even a pro trying to grow?

The first thing has to be the first thing, like how we have to pick our leaf, water, or fire starter before we go into the long grass. We have to know our games for real and not just hack and pretend like a n00b, and we need to go over what it means to actually be a Christian, not just someone who thinks they are a Christian or is pretending to be a Christian. This chapter may make some of us feel like hitting the skip button, thinking it's the annoying tutorial in a game we've already played a hundred times, and we're saying to ourselves, "Yes, yes, I'm a prisoner, he's from that town, he's the rebel leader, we're going to an execution, can I skip to the character creation menu now?"

I understand if you are feeling like that, but we can't just hit B-A-R-R-Y and skip it like a level in the SNES Lion King Game, and we can't just load an older sibling's save file and play from there (not that I did that, but my little brother did that to get past a certain water temple fairly often). I hope you read this chapter just as well as any other because as Philippians 2:12 says "Work out [our] own salvation with fear and trembling" before we get into the deeper issues. So, without dragging it out like an unskippable credit reel, or making you wait like a Half-Life 3 fan, let's get into it.

Before you get into a book about knowing God better, the first question is if you really know him in the first place. And I don't mean you think there may be some higher power or that you attend a church on Christmas and Easter and when your mom promises to go to the game store afterward if you attend. This is important because there's a common problem with many people who think they are a Christian and maybe have said a prayer without knowing what they were doing or really meaning it. Jesus puts this into example in Matthew 7:21–23, "Not everyone who says to me 'Lord, Lord' will enter the kingdom of heaven but the one who does the will of my Father who is in heaven. On that day many will say to me, 'Lord, Lord, did we not prophesy in your name and cast out demons in your name and do many mighty works in your name?' And then will I declare to them, 'I never knew you, depart from me, you workers of lawlessness.'"

I don't want anyone to get confused about this, no one is saved by works, even by a "sinner's prayer." The people in this passage are clearly relying on what they DID for Jesus rather than being IN Jesus. This is the important difference. We are saved by *grace* through *faith* rather than anything we say or do for Jesus. We can say a prayer or be a pastor and still be out if those are the things we're banking on.

A prayer can express our faith in Christ, but that's not the thing that saved us.

Another thing that can't save us is just "going to church." One unique thing about Christianity is that it's the only "religion" that we can't actually be born into. While some people claim it by birth, and even some countries try to base our Christianity by birth, we can only become a Christian by believing in Christ. We can't just push up, up, down, down, left, right, left, right, B, A to get our life right. To use a classic example: going to church and using that as the basis for our Christian claim is like going into a garage and claiming it makes us a car. We can do it, but it doesn't make it true, nor does it do anything for our horsepower. To use a video game example: we can be playing every Gran Turismo and F1 racing game there is every day of our life, but it doesn't make us a professional racer in real life.

Even if our great-grandparents were the founding couple of a church, built the church with their own hands, and then our grandparents and parents were all pastors and deacons of the church, and a million people got saved by their work all over the world. That doesn't save us, and to rely on it makes as much sense as Kratos being able to destroy armies and monsters and pantheons but can't break a rotting wooden door. Even if you enjoyed listening to them every Sunday, Sunday night, Tuesday night prayer meeting, and Wednesday night service, that's not what does it. Nor does sitting in one of their pews save you even if it's comfortable and you sat in the same spot your whole life. The only thing that saves is *grace* through *faith.* We can't just do things we think are good and expect them to be added up like gold coins until our red-hatted character (and his underappreciated green-hatted brother) get an extra life in Heaven.

As Romans 10:9–13 says, "If you confess with your mouth that Jesus is Lord and believe in your heart that God raised him from the dead, you will be saved. For with the heart one believes and is justified and with the mouth one confesses and is saved. For the Scripture says, 'Everyone who believes in him will not be put to shame.' For there is no distinction between Jew and Greek; for the same Lord is Lord of all, bestowing his riches on all who call on him. For 'everyone who calls on the name of the Lord will be saved.'"

This doesn't mean we'll be perfect, but it means we genuinely believe in God and Jesus Christ for salvation, that's what saves us. Not doing specific things or "playing the right games" or "having the right system." And it's important to check on ourselves from time to time if we've had that moment of faith, belief, and confession or not. Some of us have believed but never confessed, and some have confessed without ever believing. Both are lacking without the other. We can know the entire game's player's guide like the back of our hand. But we've got to press "start" to say we've played it.

You may be wondering why this is so important to start with salvation while many of you reading this book have been saved for a long time, and some of you may have been saved for so long you don't even remember when or how you got saved. But that's why we can't just skip ahead to more traditional "Bible study tips" and how to play video games with some Christian elements and how to reply to people who think all video games are bad.

1 John 2:19 may show you why we must start at this point: "They went out from us, but they were not of us for if they had been

of us, they would have continued with us. But they went out, that it might become plain that they all are not of us."

This happens all too often. Many of you may have seen it yourselves.

Some of you may even feel like you're close to being one of these people, and some of you have already become one and you're just reading this because your parent / friend / significant other got this for you and you're humoring them and are curious if I'm going to reference a specific game you like. But that's why it's so important to ask yourself if you've ever gotten to the point where you've accepted Christ as your savior and received his offer of salvation for yourself. It can't start anywhere else. 2 Corinthians 13:5 tells us, "Examine yourselves, to see whether you are in the faith. Test yourselves. Or do you not realize this about yourselves that Jesus Christ is in you?—unless indeed you fail to meet the test!"

I would hate for you to go through a book on finding God in your video games while you miss finding God himself, failing the test when it's time to meet Jesus. That would be as bad as spending your entire time in a racing game going the wrong way down the track, you just can't win the race. And since we have one life to live and we never know when it's going to be over, we don't want to miss our chance at salvation forever, like a Fallout 3 bobblehead or the Nahkriin mask in Skyrim. So, I want to ask you a second time.

Are you a spiritual n00b, a newb, or even a pro trying to grow?

If you've never chosen to follow Christ. You need to start with that. We have all sinned from little things, like stealing someone's sweet roll, to medium things, like testing if friendly fire is on in a game by shooting the AI on our team, all the way to something as big as assassinating a templar grandmaster. That sin puts us apart from God because he is holy, without sin, and can't let any sin into his kingdom. God could have left us this way. But he doesn't think of us as a Heartless or a Nobody. God loved us so much that he sent his Son Jesus to live here (John 3:16). Jesus lived without ever sinning then gave himself as a sacrifice for our sins when we deserved our penalty. He died on the cross but then rose again on the third day. He's coming again, and however long we have until then, including if that means we die before he returns. That gives us a choice which faction we'll join, his or our own. Without him, we can't win, and there's no hope, joy, or life without him. As far as we get and as hard as we try, we can't get there on our own. All our good works are crushed by the weight of our bad deeds, and those good deeds become as useful as a simple elixir at the end battle of a Final Fantasy game (we have 99 and use 0) or a flamethrower in Dead Space (can't actually destroy the enemy, just makes them on fire while coming toward us).

Even if some movies and video games make it look like hell is some kingdom of Satan where he's the king or the boss, he's going down into the lake of fire to suffer just like those without Christ (Revelation 20:7–15). Without him, all anyone will feel when he returns is that same panic of playing for ten hours without saving and then the screen freezes or when our system gets the red ring of death and we don't have a backup.

This is your chance to accept him and forever have your name in the Book of Life by trusting in him, not your own works or anything else. Make that choice to follow Jesus because (a) you'll never regret it, and (b) your life is like a cutscene with the chance to accept Jesus being a quick-time event that you never know when the prompt will disappear, and it'll be too late. Choose him today; you can pray, but that prayer only saves if you believe and confess him. If that's you. Congratulations on joining God's family! Please, find a church to keep growing, and let me know this book has helped you in that! Don't stop now, keep reading because the rest of this book will help you in the steps after this one! Our relationship with God is worth the effort more than Dead Space's hand cannon so we can't take it for granted.

If you know you've truly believed in and confessed Christ but it's been so long ago you barely remember it or you've never really done anything with Jesus after that time, then I'm glad you're here reading this because I'd like to help you get beyond that into the more awesome and deeper life Christ has for you! For some of you, salvation may have that feeling of needing to save again after you just saved or reload your clip when you've only shot one bullet, and you may have gone down to an altar so many times to be sure. That's okay also, we'll talk about how we can feel that assurance that it happened later! But like an open-world game that you can play for years and find new things, God always has more for you to discover about him. Get ready to hear a lot of things; some will make you say "Amen!" and some may make you say "ouch," but I encourage you to keep reading with an open mind because the results are worth it!

If you know you've been saved but someone hurt you and you've turned away from "Christians" and "like Christ but not believers" and are less than enthusiastic about life in Christ, don't let someone else stand in the way of you growing in Christ and getting all that he has in store for you through this book. Even "Christians" will hurt us because some of them mean well but aren't very good at living for Christ yet, and some of them try hard but mess up and don't know that they need to be saying sorry for the times they are making Jesus look bad, and some even aren't really Christians in the first place but are claiming to be Christians because they're not "anything else." We shouldn't be surprised when these people hurt us and cause Jesus to look bad or mistake them for God himself is treating us poorly; 2 Corinthians 11:14–15 puts it this way, "And no wonder, for even Satan disguises himself as an angel of light. So, it is no surprise if his servants, also, disguise themselves as servants of righteousness. Their end will correspond to their deeds." So, we can't let what others do "in the name of Christ" get in the way of us and Christ if it is unbiblical because they will get dealt with, and we don't want to get into the same boat as theirs because of what they did to us. That'd be as bad as being shocked at how bad the logic of the bad guy's plan is so you join his team!

If you know you've truly believed in and confessed Christ and are actively growing in him and love him, then I hope this book will still give you some fresh insight, help, motivation, and methods in getting further in your journey with Christ. Even if thinking about God gives you that feeling of safety of getting online in StarCraft and seeing a bunch of Korean words in your team's chat, all our spiritual lives could use some additional pylons, so this can be your minerals and vespene gas.

If you happen to be a gamer who got this book as a gift for Christmas, birthday, graduation or someone got it for you in the checkout line because they saw video game words in it and you're reading this begrudgingly, thanks for getting this far! Consider this an achievement unlocked, but it's not time for the end credits yet! I hope you keep reading and are ready to learn but also get some fun game references and some funny anecdotes. On the bright side, I'll try not to repeat too much of it like a character you accidentally talked to again after exiting a long and drawn-out dialogue. But it's important to get these things down because your spiritual life is not Yojimbo, you can't just throw money at it and win.

If you're a relative who's reading this to try to understand video games and if they are something that will bring your relative closer to Jesus or further away, I hope you will see the good parts of games and what they CAN be for those who know Jesus and want to follow him even while enjoying video games a lot. I hope you can understand the points of the book, even with the game references you may not quite understand, and God will help your relationship with him as well through it!

Some of you may be wondering why video games are still even okay to play with some of the content in them, and that's okay to ask. While there's some things we'll cover later about certain types of games, God often uses things people naturally enjoy to reach them with his Word, and video games are no exception.

Once we get salvation settled, and we know who we are actually in Christ, we can move on to who we are in Christ and see if we have hit that "start button" on our relationship with God.

Chapter Questions

1. Would you say you have a relationship with God? Are you a spiritual n00b, a newb, or even a pro trying to grow?
2. If yes, where would you put that relationship on a scale of novice to master?
3. What is something you're hoping to get from this book?
4. How often do you honestly think about God while you're playing video games?
5. Are you ready to push "start"?

Achievement Unlocked:
NOT A N00B

CHAPTER 2

The Start Button on Your Relationship with God

There's nothing like turning on a game system, inserting a new game (or selecting the downloaded file), then watching an opening sequence before finally hitting the start button. It's a moment of anticipation and excitement, and that opening can make your day and become a momentous part of your life that sticks with you as the first time you began an awesome game.

The sound of galloping of hooves, a piano comes in with rising notes in quick succession followed by a slow drop from a violin, a moon descends in the darkness over a hero in a green tunic riding a horse that was the source of the galloping sound, a shield with the words "The Legend of Zelda: Ocarina of Time" flashes across the screen, inviting us to press start. This is one such opening that has stuck with me and still brings a feeling of excitement. Similarly, the first time I saw a chess match between two kings transform into live fighting between armies, escalating as the pieces move and take each other, finishing with one soldier letting the king fall and the words "Age of Empires II: Age of Kings" flashing into view. And who could forget the first time hearing the sad piano music beginning as characters sit around a fire, with a character with blond hair looking out over ruins and saying, "Listen to my story. This...may be our last chance" in Final Fantasy X. These stuck with me personally, and I know we could spend a long time talking about other similar examples given the chance.

Other games have a great opening when they are first started, but either from the beginning or slowly over the game, you realize that the game is not worth the time it takes to play or the money you spent. The game feels boring, the challenges aren't that hard, the plot is missing in depth, the characters aren't interesting, the quests don't feel like they're worth the time to complete them. You find yourself shelving it and wishing you never bought it or promptly taking it to trade in for another game, even if they only give you partial credit because you forgot the receipt.

That's like salvation for some. Some of us never lost our sense of excitement and have been following God strongly for a long time, and like those classic games, we enjoy God and all he has to offer. Others of us, when we first get saved, we usually have some great sense of feeling of something great beginning and hope. But then for many, that's where the excitement and hope ended as well. Some of us may have gone to a church that was filled with people who claimed Christ but acted exactly the opposite of what the Bible says and left us feeling like maybe the whole thing was a mistake to get involved in and that Jesus just might be as (spoiler alert for Bioshock) fake as "Atlas" (the good news is Jesus is definitely not fake). Some of us just got bored from a church staler and more predictable than a game of Pong and more tedious than when a download goes from six minutes left to twenty hours left, and now we don't see anything exciting to fuss about in God. Some of us were happy to get saved but got involved in things we'd avoid posting on public forums, and our conscience has been seared to the point of barely wanting to listen to God's Word so we won't feel guilty. Then we end up treating the things of God like bad guys we need to hide in a cardboard box from, hoping an exclamation mark doesn't pop up over their heads instead of looking at them like the shield that keeps Satan from no-scope headshotting you.

Some of us have been to countless camps and church events and revivals, prayed for deliverance, breakthrough, joy, hope, or help, and only later to have felt like nothing has helped. Then the numbness and apathy set in, at least in our heart and mind if not in our words and actions yet. God began to feel as far off as a canceled sequel or as far off as playing for days to finish a game and unlock everything, then the completion percentage shows up as only 4 percent.

Whatever way the joy and excitement died out for some of us, that's not where it should end. We were not made to lose our joy and purpose and were not made to have as hard a time as beating F-Zero GX in Master Class. God wants us to get it back, have it, and keep it.

To put it into perspective: God didn't want us to be NPCs just walking about on our daily course, sitting in the same places at the same times of day, with the same dialogue options with the other NPCs. We shouldn't just wait to give a quest or an item to another person, thinking, *I'm not a pastor or a famous speaker or a theologian, so I don't need to really get that deep into God.* God made us to be a main character in his story, to help him save the universe, save the galaxy, save the world, and save the people around us from their apathy that traps them and keeps them apart from real life and from their sins that keep them controlled like people with headcrabs. Whatever your needs are, Jesus is the answer. Beyond our cultures, beyond our preferences, it's his message that changes things.

If any of us have put away the "game" of our relationship with God, it's time to turn it back on and hit the start button. This is our chance to try a different cause for a different effect. Consider this our tutorial to make the game make more sense so we can win it this time. A chance to have a better ending than an NPC in Silent Hill (or really almost any ending in Silent Hill). And even if we feel like we never lost that sense of joy and purpose, these are the same principles to grow in that relationship even deeper.

While there are many times that we may have made a choice to follow Jesus, follow him better, or rededicate ourselves to him, we may have found shortly after that we fell right back into old habits, old patterns, and old sins that rob us of our assurance of salvation. This is because change and growth require two parts, but most people don't know or forget to tell us about that second part for whatever reason. Kind of like someone who forgets to tell us that level or that quest item we've been looking all over for is only found when we update the game or download the DLC or get the expansion pack.

The first part is to choose to follow God better *TODAY*.

We may have chosen that multiple times, but it's an important step. To push that start button even if the game has been difficult before. Because failing to make that choice ends up being sadder than when we realized we were fighting Roxas and realizing we were making some less than good choices in the Shadow of the Colossus combined. Some of us even have restarted our file multiple times to make sure we started the game better in the first place because we weren't happy with our current file or made worse choices than a beginner in Fallout choosing melee perks.

For some, this is the hardest part. Maybe there has been a lot of reasons for us to resist making that choice to do so, either because of past experiences or because of fear of what it entails, but it is something that will be infinitely worth it when we decide we're ready to follow God better, no matter where you'd personally put yourself on the spectrum of "close to God" or "he's way off in the distance somewhere that direction but the graphics aren't even picking him up beyond some blocky structure on the horizon." We can't just keep Jesus at maximum melee range; we need him with us every step of the way. The Bible even says "Now is the favorable time; behold, now is the day of salvation" (2 Corinthians 6:2), so don't let today go by when we're not promised anything beyond what we're doing right this second.

So, whatever we need to do, and however we need to do it, we can take the time to go ahead and make that decision right now to follow God better. Even if we're not confident in our ability to see that choice through, we need to keep reading this book with that decision already being made in our minds. Finish this tutorial, beat the level-one bad guys, and we'll get into the further levels, learning as we go and getting extra tutorials on our abilities as we run into those situations.

The second part is to choose to follow God better *DAILY*.

As long as we think doing it one time is "good enough," we won't find progress very quickly, if ever. Reloading a save file only gets us back where we saved, it doesn't make us progress in the game. And anyone who has played Animal Crossing knows this: leaving our game frozen for a long time doesn't mean nothing changes, it leaves cockroaches multiplying and residents leaving town. In our spiritual life, those residents are our progress in faith, and the cockroaches are things that are better out of our lives. This is that part many people forget to tell us about in spiritual growth. Some seem to honestly believe that we just need to REALLY mean it when we pray for the first time, and all the issues with our relationship with God will forever be smooth sailing. That advice shows that they're probably a n00b or just mistaken because no one genuinely playing a game finds the whole game as easy as pressing start. For an example of that, Paul describes his own save file in Philippians 3:12–15:

> Not that I have already obtained this or am already perfect, but I press on to make it my own because Christ Jesus has made me his own. Brothers, I do not consider that I have made it my own. But one thing I do: forgetting what lies behind and straining forward to what lies ahead, I press on toward the goal for the prize of the upward call of God in Christ Jesus. Let those of us who are mature think this way, and if in anything you think otherwise, God will reveal that also to you.

Paul knew that there's not one moment we "have it together" but that it was a daily action of pressing on daily toward Christ. And that's the same for us! We may feel like there's so many things between us and Christ that we can't even decide on where to start to get the relationship on track, but Paul's whole point is to pick a direction that's toward Jesus and go! Put a rubber band around the directional pad if you have to so you can keep heading in the right direction, but keep moving!

We'll go through some common issues together in the next few chapters, and there's a list of resources for more if the ones we find don't address the things we feel hold us back. Make that choice TODAY, and from there, make that choice DAILY. That's what makes the difference so that even if we fail in a big way, we know we're not abandoned by God, and we don't lose our entire assurance of salvation, because we've been following him up to right now, and we know him enough to run to him with our sins instead of away from him and hiding. That gets us right back on the track and keeps us from getting tossed around or losing from sitting still too long like a level in Sonic so he just leaves or Mario losing a life from a timer getting to zero or getting Wolverine blown up by an android because we forgot to pause when we went to grab an energy drink (or our older sibling unpaused it so the timer would run out while we were gone so it would be their turn, even though we KNOW we paused it…but I digress).

Here's an example of choosing to try TODAY and DAILY from my video gaming. When the first Halo game came out, I was obsessed with getting every single achievement in solo mode. We had no internet or second controller, so the multiplayer ones were out of reach, but it was my mission in life to get all the ones I possibly could get my hands on. To do that meant playing through the game on Legendary Mode. I was not a great shot when I first tried it, and I had to stop playing a lot and restart from save files, but I was not about to quit over something as trivial as that. I remember the feeling of panic as I ran backward, jumping and shooting at Flood, used the pistol-whip attack on countless sleeping Grunts and Jackals, and played it so much I was fighting in my dreams and hearing the sounds and music even when the volume was off. But finally, I got to the final level, riding a Warthog across an exploding ship and was using every ounce of self-control to not throw the control the uncountable times I fell off a cliff or exploded. But I practiced daily and daily got further. After hours and hours, I finally heard that sweet, sweet sound of an achievement being unlocked. We think of this in games, but strangely, we often find ourselves quitting on the harder things in life when the same amount of perseverance could make all the difference.

And here's an example of choosing to try TODAY and DAILY from outside video games. I got saved in early high school, and I was taught that if I had some issues with my spiritual growth, it was because I didn't choose TODAY correctly or didn't "have enough faith." So, I would weekly choose TODAY to follow God right and better, and then wonder why I had to do it again the next week because I had hit a wall through the week (and to be honest, sometimes the wall was the next day). That made me slip into choosing it monthly because it was too guilt-inducing, then that led to choosing just at special revivals or camps where the speaker and the music lined up was just right. But when I realized the TODAY choice needed to be balanced by making the choice DAILY, it made me grow a lot faster, and the issues that I encountered were easier to overcome by the fact that I had chosen each day to follow God better. It was much easier to deal with temptations when I had made the choice that day rather than trying to remember the feelings I had when I made the choice several weeks ago at some big event. And after that realization, my trips to the altar were to thank him or ask for help for a specific thing rather than to shake the feeling of needing to "get saved" or "rededicate" again just to make sure.

So, take the time right now to make that choice. Make the decision to choose to follow God better TODAY, and make the decision to choose to follow God DAILY. Do what you need to do to make those choices and show yourself you've hit start. Get baptized, take communion, tell your friends/coworkers you're a Christian, find a church, join a new believer's class or a small group, and clean out certain things from your life God's been putting on your heart but you've been putting off. To give a Minecraft example: change it to survival mode already, and start making something. Then get ready to design your character.

Your Relationship with God

‹ PRESS START ›

Chapter Questions

1. Have you ever hit roadblocks in your faith that made you feel like you just weren't trying hard enough?
2. Which do you have a harder time remembering, to choose to follow Christ TODAY or DAILY?
3. Which video game(s) do you remember the best when you first pushed the start button?
4. Will you make the choice to follow God better TODAY right now?
5. How will you remind yourself to follow God better DAILY?

Achievement Unlocked:
AND THEY'RE OFF

CHAPTER 3

Designing Your Character

Some of my favorite games start with designing my character. And while that looks different across systems and individual games, there are some similarities that tie it all together. The ability to customize your character and choose how he/she/it will look is a thread that draws many people to games. Some games just let you do their skill sets, some include things like clothing, gender, hair, character type, alignment, and even some get down to facial features. Even in games where the main character can't be customized, the beginning where you get to know your character can make or break a game.

"I'm a person, not a video game character, I can't 'customize my character' in real life!" I can already hear some of you saying. And you're right in the sense that we can't alter our race, face, height, and many other facets about ourselves without some kind of surgery. You also can't necessarily choose a class and skills that go with it, like being naturally better at stealth or two-handed weapons. I get that. But what if I told you that you can alter your real-life "character" in some very surprising ways?

Let me explain. You have some things that you can't change for sure. You can't change your race, where you were born, who your parents were, how you grew up to this current point, or the decisions that you made up to this current point. But just like how you can't decide your in-game character woke up in a prison (again!), then you make choices that follow that event; your real-life character can change from this point on and be customized based on what kind of person you want to be and what kind of effort you want to put into "leveling up" yourself.

To set up some base things, we're going to look at who you are now.

Some of you were hoping I'd ignore that question because your actions up to this point would be a save file you'd personally like to delete. But here we are. And I want to give you some encouragement in that department: you may very well not be who you think you are.

If you've gotten to this point without being a believer in Christ, then (a) thanks for reading this far anyway! (b) you need to settle that part before any of this (outside the game references) will make sense and be able to apply to you. I encourage you to go back to chapter 1 and get that settled.

If you're continuing to this point, I'm going to assume you've settled the matter, know you're a believer in Christ for sure, and are ready for it.

Believers sometimes make bad choices. Sometimes, believers act like anything but a believer in Jesus Christ. And that causes a lot of people new in the faith to get turned off to following Christ and makes a lot of people who are not Christians add it to their "reasons for unbelief." I understand that happens, but I want to remind you of two things: (1) you can be saved and not be perfect, that's actually the point, BUT (2) if you're a Christian who, as a habit, is never acting like a follower of Jesus, then there's something majorly wrong with that and you need to evaluate your beliefs. If you genuinely believe but have a hard time not sinning, we'll cover that a little later. But as a genuine believer, you have two realities going on, justification and sanctification. They make the Christian life seem confusing but a lot simpler when we look at it this way:

Before we accept Christ, all our best works are being canceled out by the bad things we do, and we end up with 0 percent holiness because of our sins (Romans 3:9–20). In case any of us forgot, sin is anything we think, say, or do that does not make God happy. When we accept Christ, we get justified. That means our position with God is set, and our holiness in his eyes is 100 percent, and why when we die, we can be with him based on our relationship with him positionally. This isn't a glitch, it's God applying his Son's righteousness to us (Romans 3:23–24). It's a little like a friend letting us use his 100 percent file to stop someone hating on us (of course, it's very different, but that example might help get the point across).

The issue for most of us though is the second part, sanctification. Sanctification is our practical relationship with God, and it fluctuates depending on if we are walking in the flesh or in the Spirit (Galatians 5). Because of Christ, we can never get back down to 0 percent righteous, but because of him being very gracious to us, we can sometimes get ourselves as close as possible, and it's only that grace that's keeping us from 0 percent again. The opposite of that is true as well, the more like Christ we live and walk, the higher we get, but because we live in a world with sin, we won't get to 100 percent holy until we are with him in a new heaven and a new earth (Revelation 20–21). Like a game with radiant quests but isn't open-ended, there's always something more to work on until the game itself is done (though it's actually going to be a more awesome than imaginable sequel).

So, the question is, what are our characters like?

To answer that question, we need to break it down into two realms. The first one is on God's side, the second is on our side.

The first question is, who did God make you to be?

Whether we are aware of (or are living up to) the following attributes, there are several things that are part of our characters' skill sets that are part of us in Christ automatically. Like how certain races in RPGs have bonus perks or enhanced skills, we have things built in us. And while Galatians 5 shows us that we may not be walking in them as we should, they are still a part of us to walk in. While that list is easy for us to read ourselves (and I encourage you to read that entire chapter as soon as you finish this chapter), I wanted to make another list from other verses to show how we are made. This is not an exhaustive list, but these are all things that are part of our character by our justification. One way you could think about it is like a fighting game combo, if you don't hit the right buttons in the right order, you may never know you were able to use that move.

1. God made us to worship him. It's one of the things we'll be doing for eternity, and it's something we're supposed to start knowing. Our character should be known for our worship, whatever type of worship music and whatever expression that looks like, it should be toward God and honoring him (Revelation 7:9).
2. God made us to walk in the light. Even if some of us feel like we enjoy the darker things in life more, that's not what our characters are designed for. It's like trying to siege a castle with skirmishers, going against an entire enemy team in Modern Warfare with just a .357 Magnum, going against the Eagles with the second-string Dolphins in Madden '20, or fighting Sephiroth with only Cait Sith. Some of us try to be in as little light as possible, but it hurts us more than we know by going against our own character in Christ (1 John 1:7).
3. God made us to be holy. While sometimes it seems like the last thing we can be, for some of us at times the last thing we would even WANT to be. But to whatever degree we'd like it, we are made to be holy. That's why we have a conscience that cries out when we go against it, and why even when we do things that deafen that conscience, we can't get rid of it (1 Peter 1:15).
4. God made us to do good works. We know how to solve difficult puzzles, encircle enemy teams, unlock weapons and skills, and beat pretty much any enemy that comes our way. But when it comes to the real world, sometimes there's a harder time putting those good works to practice. If we can save countless worlds in video games, it's good to know that God also made us to do things to make this world better as well with our work if we follow our character design (Ephesians 2:10).

5. God made us to be a new creation. When we got saved, that changed us. If you ever wondered why it was so hard to live the Christian life, it's because now you have two natures that are working against each other. It's like how it's hard to level up two opposing skills at the same time. We spend a lot of our experience points and time on things that hurt our new nature rather than build it up. But part of our character is that we aren't who we were before and can't let ourselves continue to act like it (2 Corinthians 5:17).
6. God made us to be ambassadors. We are supposed to represent him to others. This job gets harder sometimes when we lose our cool while gaming and yell and curse out people a thousand miles away. And while we think it's okay sometimes because they don't know who we are to know we are Christians to make him look bad, he knows we're wasting opportunities and missing chances to tell them who we really are (2 Corinthians 5:20–21).
7. God made us to tell others about Jesus so they can know him. As awkward as you might feel sharing the gospel, and is probably the reason many of us do it very seldomly or don't do it at all, it's part of our character design. Some of us feel like, as gamers, we don't interact with people enough to even share our faith, but the online gaming community is huge, and while online games may not be your forte, there are some games you probably play online and game stores you go to in order to get new games and merch. We're around a lot more people and in contact with more people than we think (Matthew 28:18–20).
8. God made us a temple. Part of our stats are that we are also a place of worship. That's why Christianity has a personal aspect as well as a corporate aspect. We are designed to worship God by ourselves as well as in a community. Paul even says that's one of the reasons to avoid certain sins because they are against ourselves and that means against God's temple (1 Corinthians 6:20).

9. God made us so that we can do everything for his glory. Of all the beings our characters in games are designed to serve, worship, glorify, quest for, etc., our real characters are designed to do everything we do for God's glory. As much as it seems like it'd be difficult to kill zombies or do some quests in your games for God's glory, just wait, we'll get to how to do that a few chapters down the road (1 Corinthians 10:31).
10. God made us to be thankful. While it seems like an odd thing to be made for, we are created by God to be thankful. Thankfulness is an important part of our character stats because it makes the difference between being self-centered (we've all met self-centered people, and none of them are pleasant if we're honest) or seeing how everything God gives us is a gift we don't deserve. A variation of the word "thank" shows up more than 150 times in the Bible, and very often, it is a command, and that itself shows how important God thinks it is (Psalm 7:17, Psalm 30:4, 1 Thessalonians 5:18).

If we feel overwhelmed by our character stats, and like it's too hard to remember them all at this point, we don't need to panic! We need to remember at the beginning of any RPG, our stats are confusing, we have to figure out the level-up system, and there's a learning curve because we don't know the plot and who we are yet. God gives us time to grow into who we really are because he loves us exactly where we are but loves us way too much to let us stay there. Like how we enjoy our character at the start of a game but can't stay fighting rats with simple clothes and expect to win the game.

The second question is, who do you want to be?

We spend a lot of time customizing our characters in games, but what about our own character? Who do we really want to be in this life? We may have had a lot working against us in life, and I don't know your whole story, but however we got to wherever we are right now doesn't change that we're here right now. Because we're here, we have a choice in a lot of what our future will be. We have a choice in what we do with who we become. We have a choice in how we will spend your free time, in what you learn, and in what we apply to raise our character's stats. Even if we had the worst start imaginable, we have a chance to make the rest of our game different. So, it's important to decide what work we put into your character, just like we can't expect to beat the end boss right at the beginning of the game, and we have to put the work into leveling up our in-game characters.

This part is more up to us. We now know at least ten ways God designed our character, but what else do we want to put into our character? While we can't give ourselves magic and can't jump over and over again and expect to jump over buildings, there's a lot more in our control than we realize. And since we don't want to put all our skill points into weapons only for there to be an unskippable stealth mission, we need to look into God's Word for what kinds of skills we should be investing our time into.

Let's look at the "Fruit of the Spirit" in Ephesians 5:22–23 as an example. Some of us know them by heart and can sing the song, but in case you forgot or never heard of them, the Bible says, "The fruit of the Spirit is love, joy, peace, patience, kindness, goodness, faithfulness, gentleness, self-control." These are all stats we have, believe it or not. And while you may have heard of them as a list of things to "work harder to have," they are actually a list of things we have as believers already. They are the fruit of the Spirit, and all believers have the Holy Spirit in them (Ephesians 1:13, 4:30). So, they are not things we need to "work harder to have" but rather things we already have but need to choose to walk in.

Looking at that list, I don't know anyone who wouldn't think the world would be better if everyone was more loving, more joyful, more peaceful, more patient, kinder, better, more faithful, gentler, and having more self-control. Sometimes we feel like saying, "Okay, I *may* have these in Christ, but those skills are definitely in the novice range," which may be true for you. But remember how skills in games get leveled up: you need to level yourself up or use the skill until it levels up.

STRENGTH:	20
AGILITY:	17
WISDOM:	23
ATTACK:	21
DEFENSE:	19
MAX HP:	109
EXP:	3200
LOVE:	22
JOY:	25
PEACE:	19
PATIENCE:	5
SELF-CONTROL:	3

How do we level ourselves up? By getting into God's Word and applying what it says in our life.

How do we level that skill up? When we have a chance to use that aspect of the fruit, we choose to use it instead of choosing or reacting in the opposite; remember we are patient instead of being impatient, remember we are kind instead of responding unkindly. We have to make a choice as to who we want to be.

For an example from my video games: When I first played Final Fantasy IX, I was so excited by the story and what happened next that I sprinted through bad guy fights and didn't save my gil and didn't think about switching out party members, so before long, I was constantly getting beaten, and it took forever to go back and find bad guys I could beat to level up enough to not get beaten constantly.

For an example in my life: Patience is something that, since I became a Christian, was much easier for me than self-control, so I gave myself a pass on self-control because most people find patience a much more difficult prospect. This didn't help me get more self-control though, and I kept running into issues with self-control until I realized it was already mine in Christ, stopped using excuses for it, and chose it over lack of control when it came to it. Not that I always chose it, like an older RPG where our spell casting, attacks, and blocks can fail, I do at times as well, but I kept working on it to level it up and chose what's already mine when the situations arise.

So, who did God make us to be?

Who do we want to be?

And now that we have a few of those answers, how do we get to the point where the answers to those questions are a reality?

Later on in Galatians, Paul gives us the answer, "Do not be deceived: God is not mocked; for whatever one sows, that he will also reap. For the one who sows to his own flesh will from the flesh reap corruption, but the one who sows to the Spirit will from the Spirit reap eternal life" (chapter 6:7–8).

Note the choices here.

Walking in the flesh reaps corruption, not eternal death because those in Christ are his. But corruption isn't something to ignore and say, "Well I'm saved, so I can do whatever I want." Corruption hurts us personally, hurts our relationship with God, hurts those around us who are Christians, and hurts those who don't believe in Christ and that corruption makes them feel justified in that unbelief. It's not something to ignore like an annoying fetch quest item we don't feel like returning, so keep almost indefinitely without it ever affecting us. It goes against our nature, so sowing in the flesh causes carnage to our character stats, hurts our conscience, and ripples out to others.

Walking in the Spirit reaps eternal life. This is interesting to note that it doesn't mean our good works save us as that would go against the whole rest of Galatians. But the thing about eternal life is that we get eternal life at salvation, it's not something that happens after death (1 Timothy 6:12). Eternal life starts at salvation, but the closer to Christ we get, the more we experience that eternal life on this side of it. And that's not something we should be like, "Well, I don't mind waiting until I die to have eternal life, I just want to have fun." But that misses the fact that reaping eternal life isn't some spiritual cosmic idea, it impacts our daily lives as we interact with our world, and the more like Christ we are, the more we can handle the fallen world in a way that helps our conscience and helps make the world better rather than worse.

These are very simple to understand with the agriculture example of sowing and reaping, and even if we've never had a farm or a garden, we've probably at least played a game with farming in it at one point or another. So, if we put corn in the ground and we expect to get apples, we'd get some more-than-confused looks from others. And the same is true for video game examples; we can't expect to level up our destruction magic while only using a bow, we can't do a special move in a fighting game if we put the wrong button combo in, and we can't expect to win a king-of-the-hill match if we stay at our spawn points. So, we can't expect to put sin into our lives constantly and expect to get God, his plans, his goodness, and his character.

Even if the details of where to go are hard to know right now, when we know what our character is supposed to be, it makes the path ahead easier. Being who we are made to be is like a checkpoint that activates a quest marker on our map. We can't expect for God to tell us where to go while we are completely ignoring everything else he's saying, so we need to start with simply listening to who he's saying we are and what he's saying we're like. Like Jeremiah 6:16 says, "Thus says the Lord: 'Stand by the roads, and look, and ask for the ancient paths, where the good way is and walk in it and find rest for your souls.'" So we don't end up like the people at the end of the verse: "But they said, 'We will not walk in it.'"

There's also gifts that God designed us with, given to us by the Holy Spirit, but those are for a much later chapter.

So, now we know more about how we are designed as a character and how to design our character further in the real world. We'll look at the three ways to play our "game": solo mode, hardcore mode, and co-op playing.

Chapter Questions

1. What traits do you want your real-world character to have?
2. What things do you need to start working on today so those are a reality?
3. What kind of person do you want to be?

4. Are you willing to put the same time and effort into leveling up yourself as you do a game character?
5. What aspect of the fruit of the Spirit do you find most surprising to actually have when you thought you didn't?

Achievement Unlocked:
WHO ARE YOU?

CHAPTER 4

Solo Mode

There are two basic ways to play a game, and we're going to look first at solo mode. In some games, this can be the only way to play, and in other games, it's the main quest with multiplayer being more like a separate game, and in other games there isn't a solo mode. In our study, solo mode is the personal and private part of our spiritual walk with God. And while it's the only part many people think about, it's actually only half of our walk with God. Since both are important, we need to play both aspects of the "game."

It's like if we're not currently playing our file, our in-game character won't be going anywhere or changing at all, and the world would never get saved, and we certainly won't level up. Or for a non-video game example: It's like a tree, being a Christian means we're either growing, in a state of stress that is keeping us from growing well, or dead. Solo mode has a lot of different ways to play, and all of them help us to level up as we go. There's a lot of different ways to play, and while there's no player's guide that can tell us specifically every decision we'll encounter and every dialogue option we should pick, there's principles that can help us along the way. So we can head out into the open world that is our lives with God at our side and confidence in our inventory, along with the right waypoints.

The question is, how do we go through solo mode in this life?

The answer can be broken down into two sections that will equip us to know how to make the right choices as we go through our unique solo mode. And while there are other aspects you'll encounter, these are the ways to get closer to God. As we get closer to God, it's much easier to not only know the right choices but to also make the right choices. That's the important part anyway, right? We've all been in a game where the right choice is clear, but either by our own curiosity or desire to "do it differently," we make a different choice anyway. I know personally, I've done that enough in my own life, and while it can seem like the more desirable option even for some of us at times, God's the only one who knows our character and the game's source code to know what's the right way to play. So, we need to know how to get closer to him by studying our Bible and prayer.

Studying our Bible sounds like a simple and cliché way to tell someone how to get closer to God, and if that's where we ended it, then it would be the equivalent of telling a non-gamer parent the jump button and shoot button and dropping them into the boss fight. If that was all we needed to know, a lot more Christians would be in better places spiritually. So, we're going to look at it more than just "read it."

The first part of studying our Bible is to read it daily. As anyone can tell you, it's much easier to play a game every day than to read our Bible every day. But the ease of access we have to the Bible should make them on par. The ironic thing is reading at least some of the Bible every day is such a small and simple part of our lives, but it's the first thing we drop when things get "busy." The more ironic part is that the more we read our Bible and give those other things to God, the simpler those other things get as well. And considering God is the one we are supposed to be thinking of first, and the most important thing in our lives, we need to make His word a priority, rather than something we cram into an already busy life as an afterthought to cram in or dump.

Personally, there have been times where I read my Bible frequently, and there was no competition for time between doing it and video games, I had plenty of time for both. While the times I ditched the Bible for video games and other things, I found I had less time for all of it. It's a paradox for sure, but the point of a paradox is both are true. The more time we give to God, the more time we have for other things.

The best thing about our modern society is the ease of access to the Bible. We can sync devices, set reminders, get apps. There's translations and paraphrases that make the Bible so simple we have no excuse for "not understanding it." There're even ones made animated and from Lego. So, most of the excuses for not reading our Bible start to sound more and more sad. If we're honest, usually it comes down to desire to read. Which I understand if you start at a list of "begets," but that's the great thing about the Bible. There're so many places to start! Read Joshua and Judges, and we get to imagine battles straight out of Dynasty Warriors. Read Acts, and it's like Sonic but Paul's getting people for Jesus instead of gold rings. Read Psalms, and it's like Guitar Hero with a lute. There's even plans with just a few verses from a variety of books. There're so many different places, and many of them are so simple it'd be sad if we said we couldn't understand it. We can do what we have to do to remember to read it daily.

The second part of studying our Bible is to read it for the big pictures. There's a lot of stories that connect the Bible to itself. There are big pictures of man's mistakes and God's redemption, classic stories that are important to reread because it's surprising how many parts of the story we remember halfway or incorrectly. And the big picture ideas help us to understand it when it does get confusing.

There's a lot of guides for these kinds of studies, and it takes a lot less time than reading the whole Bible if that sounds too intimidating. But basically, we just focus on the big stories of Scripture to see God's plan from our fall to his redemption. This is important because it makes it easier to know the Bible as a whole and to find things faster when you're trying to study something or find a verse on a specific topic.

For example, looking at the big picture of Romans helps you find verses and points of discussion. Romans 1:1–17 is its introduction and purpose; Romans 1:18–32 is how the pagans are sinful, Romans 2 shows how those with a moral code and the law are sinful; Romans 3 shows how all are sinful and need Jesus to save us; Romans 4 shows faith is how we are saved; Romans 5 shows how faith reunited us with God, with Adam and Jesus being examples; Romans 6 talks about how we should live because we are saved; Romans 7 shows the believer's relationship to the law; Romans 8 shows how we walk by the Spirit; Romans 9–11 shows how that salvation plays out with God's chosen people and those who have never heard; Romans 12 shows how Christians should live in response to salvation personally; Romans 13–14 shows how Christians should live in response to salvation interpersonally; Romans 15 shows how Paul has lived it out; and Romans 16 is greetings and farewells. Knowing that helps when I'm in a discussion and want to talk about justification, I can turn to Romans 3–6 for a lot of verses on it.

The third part of studying our Bible is to read it for the little details. There are so many little details in the Bible, and the only way to find them is to read something like this in hopes of finding them spelled out for you or reading it for yourself. While it's good to read the large stories, and books of the Bible, it's also important to slowly read passages for the details. This is where we can make sense of a lot of the big questions that we sometimes have because we read it too fast and miss them.

An example of this is the book of Judges. There's a LOT of confusing things about Judges, and in general, it reads like a list of what NOT to do while following God. It catches a lot of flak in general, but if you read the details, you start to see why it's so messed up; the phrase that appears twice in the book: "Everyone did what was right in his own eyes." When people do whatever they see as right instead of what God knows is right, it leads into those kinds of problems. It's interesting considering that God also used that phrase in Deuteronomy 12 to warn them that it would happen and lead to a lot of bad things. Turns out that God had the player's guide and tried to give them a spoiler alert, but they did it very wrong anyway. These little details can help us avoid the same issues in our lives and find insight into God that never gets old.

This may not seem THAT important to some, but these two parts are like playing a game we love vs. our first playthrough. Knowing the major plot can help us know where to go and what to do, and the lore can make us feel much more immersed in a game. And the little details can make or break the game; knowing the hidden paths, extra ammo, health packs, sniper spots, bad guy pop-ups, and boss weaknesses can all be what keep us alive or make us get so many game overs our controller gets in mortal danger.

An example from my life is the life of a woman I knew from when I was a missionary in Thailand. Her name was "Grandma" Lorena and was ninety-five when I left and still going strong. She read the Bible every day since she was little and always learned something from that time with God, even if it was in the little details. That's encouraging and motivating (and a little bit embarrassing at times) for me. You can relate it to games like Morrowind, Skyrim, Minecraft, or Breath of the Wild, it seems like there's always SOMETHING we never knew was there until we stumble upon it.

The fourth part of studying our Bible is to read it for theology. Please, don't stop reading here, the very word "theology" for some sounds as grating as "Hey! Listen!" and being told for the fiftieth time the batteries in your remote are nearly depleted. But that's because we forget what theology really is. Theology is simply what we believe about God but organized in a way that makes it easy to talk about. That's why reading the Bible requires theology. Any passage can add to our theology. The simple questions of "What does this passage say about God?" "What does it say about people?" "What does it say about myself?" are all how to break a passage down to learn theology. It also helps us remember what we read.

I don't know about you, but there have been plenty of times where I read the Bible, and thirty minutes later, someone asks what I read and I can't remember at all. But when I ask questions like the ones above, I learn more from that reading and remember it better later on. It helps us learn what parts of our beliefs are based on Scripture and what parts were inadvertently based on things like Assassin's Creed or Dante's Inferno. It also helps when interacting with those who don't know God because then we can remember verses that talk about specific topics as well as know what we believe when asked. Because when I was a new Christian and someone asked what I believed about God, it was hard to give a sentence answer, let alone describe him to them. But the more I read the Bible, the more I could describe God, Jesus, the Holy Spirit, sin, salvation, heaven, hell, and all the other topics that are "theology" but turn out to be important in our daily lives.

An example of this in my video gaming is the Water Temple in The Legend of Zelda: Ocarina of Time. The first few times I played through it, it took forever to get through it, and because of that I HATED it. But as I learned the little details to remember and the big picture of the game and the "theology" of the level, I grew to love it, and the last time I played through the game, I beat it so fast I reset it to play it again.

An example of this in my life is when I first became a Christian and started reading the Bible. At the time, my "theology of sin" was "if I don't get CAUGHT, it doesn't really matter what I say." So, I would say a lot of inappropriate words with my friends as long as no one "in authority" was nearby. Then one day, I read Colossians 3:8–9, "But now you must put them all away: anger, wrath, malice, slander, and obscene talk from your mouth. Do not lie to one another, seeing that you have put off the old self with its practices." Then I proceeded to say "obscene talk" about not knowing I wasn't supposed to use obscene talk previously. That's one of the purposes of the Bible when we look at 2 Timothy 3:16, "All Scripture is breathed out by God and profitable for teaching, for reproof, for correction, and for training in righteousness" It's meant to illuminate the things in our lives that are not in line with God and what we are supposed to believe, but that only happens when we read it. To help remember the Bible verses you want to study, practice a Bible verse every time you die in a game. This may mean you only practice it once in a while for some games, but if you're playing games like Star Wars Battlefront II, Dark Souls, Ghost of Tsushima, or Dead Cells, then you may be able to memorize the entire book of Psalms.

The fifth part of studying our Bible is to read it to apply. This should make sense to us, but we surprisingly often forget that the point of reading the Bible is to put what it says into practice. James 1:22–25 puts it this way, "But be doers of the word and not hearers only, deceiving yourselves. For if anyone is a hearer of the word and not a doer, he is like a man who looks intently at his natural face in a mirror. For he looks at himself and goes away and at once forgets what he was like. But the one who looks into the perfect law, the law of liberty, and perseveres, being no hearer who forgets but a doer who acts, he will be blessed in his doing."

To give some perspective, it would be like having a clear quest marker on the map and on the HUD and still running around blindly looking for where we're supposed to go. It would just be painful to watch.

Application has two aspects. The first is we have to apply it to ourselves. Nothing is sadder than God trying to tell us something and we just ignore it to say, "Wow, Dr. Robotnik really needs to hear THAT!" Our first reaction may be that, but it should remind us to check if it may apply to us as well. Like how you can't give someone tips on playing a game you've never played yourself and don't know the workings of. It takes us applying it. If we read and read without putting it into practice, it doesn't help our lives at all, and sometimes makes us more complacent about what we do because we are "at least reading our Bible every day."

As we are reminded in Matthew 7:24-27: "Everyone then who hears these words of mine and does them will be like a wise man who built his house on the rock. And the rain fell, and the floods came, and the winds blew and beat on that house, but it did not fall because it had been founded on the rock. And everyone who hears these words of mine and does not do them will be like a foolish man who built his house on the sand. And the rain fell, and the floods came, and the winds blew and beat against that house, and it fell, and great was the fall of it."

The second aspect is that we have to share what we learn. While we apply it to ourselves first, we need to learn how to share what we learn with others. Like how a good gamer tells others about the things they learn in games to help other gamers who have a harder time. It's also important to learn how to share what we learn regularly with friends and family because it helps keep us accountable to be learning ourselves. It also is a command in Colossians 3:16, "Let the word of Christ dwell in you richly, teaching and admonishing one another in all wisdom, singing psalms and hymns and spiritual songs, with thankfulness in your hearts to God." I know that sounds complicated, but really, it's just letting God's Word in us come out of us instead of forgetting it or ignoring it or hiding it.

The second section of solo mode is prayer. God's word speaks to us, and we speak back to God. Again, this sounds like a simple thing to do, but it gets surprisingly hard to get into the habit of doing without some external situation that makes us panic and pray out of need. There's a lot more to prayer than a list of people's body parts when they are sick and saying thanks before a meal or before bed. It's also more than when we are desperate and literally have no one else we can call. God is not a genie to pray to and get whatever we want, nor is he a series of console commands to get resources you need. And just because we can't see him doesn't mean he's distant and far from us, so our prayers don't really matter if we use them or not.

Prayer is talking to God. He is omnipotent (all-powerful), omnipresent (everywhere at all times), omniscient (all-knowing), and omnibenevolent (all-loving), so prayer is our connection to THAT. God isn't a cheat code to employ when things get dicey or someone we can control by asking "Would you kindly…?" It's important for us to treat God like we really believe he exists and like we really believe our relationship with him is what saves us. If we had a best friend or a significant other or a spouse, we wouldn't expect to never have any meaningful conversations with them and everything to be okay. Even in a video game, if we ghost our guild long enough, they'd boot us. We also wouldn't assume they aren't with us when we can't physically see them. So, why do we often treat God worse than them?

Psalm 145:18 says, "The Lord is near to all who call on him, to all who call on him in truth." And that's why prayer is so important for us. God gets closer to us as we speak to him. Like any relationship, communication is needed for it to grow. Even in video games, you have to enter into dialogue to gain influence with other characters, and while our prayers can never "force" God to do anything, he loves to answer us when we call. Of course, he is smarter than we are, so sometimes that answer is a "nope" or a "wait on that one," but his answers are always the best for us. That means we can trust him enough to pray, and while some may feel "if God knows what I need and my every thought, why bother praying?" To answer that, we can look at James 4:2–4, "You do not have because you do not ask. You ask and do not receive because you ask wrongly to spend it on your passions."

God values our relationship with him and wants us to communicate to Him like we would want others to do for us. We can't expect our teammate to cover us properly in a firefight if we never ask and tell our position. We can't get a quest if we never talk to the NPC who assigns quests. Communication is important in every area of life both in video games and in real life, so we can't expect to ignore communication with God. We need to pray to show our trust in God to answer.

Prayer can benefit us immensely. Because God is limitless, prayer is as limitless as his "yes." What kind of things are you asking God for yourself? What things do we need that God's waiting on us to ask? Paul prayed in Ephesians 1:15–19 over the Christians in Ephesus, and I think it shows the kinds of things we should be praying for ourselves.

> For this reason, because I have heard of your faith in the Lord Jesus and your love toward all the saints, I do not cease to give thanks for you, remembering you in my prayers, that the God of our Lord Jesus Christ, the Father of glory, may give you the Spirit of wisdom and of revelation in the knowledge of him, having the eyes of your

> hearts enlightened that you may know what is the hope to which he has called you, what are the riches of his glorious inheritance in the saints, and what is the immeasurable greatness of his power toward us who believe, according to the working of his great might.

How different would our walk with God, and our entire life, be if we had the Spirit of wisdom, the revelation in the knowledge of Jesus, the eyes of our hearts enlightened, knowing our hope to which we were called, knowing the glorious riches of our inheritance in him, and seeing the immeasurable greatness of his power toward us in our daily lives? It all starts with praying for ourselves but for the right priorities. We need to pray big because our real needs are big.

Prayer is not just for our benefit but can be beneficial for everything we do and everyone we know. What kind of things are you asking God for others? Have we subconsciously been limiting God to answer little prayers because that's all we're asking for? If God answered all our prayers, would anything be different besides a few people being a little healthier? Are we praying for the spiritual needs they have as well as the physical? To see people saved, to see lives changed, relationships healed, sad hearts overjoyed, hope restored, captives freed, the poor provided for, debts destroyed? Prayer can change so many things if we would just ask like he will answer.

This kind of prayer for others is often called intercession. It's praying for the needs of others like we would pray for our own. But the difference is that we are not just praying for physical needs like surgeries, injuries, illnesses, or financial problems but emotional needs and spiritual needs as well. We pray for those around us, those believers in other places we've heard of in trouble and danger, those who tell us their needs, even if it's over chats or talking during rounds, and for those who aren't believers to get saved. Many believers write lists of people they pray for to keep it in front of them literally so it's in front of them mentally. Personally, I've had mine in several places through the years: on my bathroom mirror, on my nightstand, next to my game system, in my Bible, on my desk, basically wherever I would see daily and use it.

One important thing in praying for others is not just saying "I'll pray for you" and then forgetting about it. It's important to note what prayers people have, remember them enough to write them down, and pray for them consistently. I recommend praying for people right away while you're talking to them when they mention something to make sure you've prayed for them even if you happen to forget later. This doesn't seem like a "normal" thing to do, but it's normal in the Bible and should be for us as believers (Acts 3:1–6, 6:5–6).

So, now that we know it's important, how do we establish a healthy and consistent habit of prayer?

The Bible shows us from the first prayers to the last that we should pray deeply and pray often. We don't need to worry if it feels like we're only praying for a short time; if you read most of the prayers in the Bible out loud, they aren't that long either. As long as those short times are frequent through the day, we will grow in our prayer habit. As you pray, you'll find that the times get longer and easier as you practice. Every drive, every lunch, every nap, every sleep, every midnight energy drink run, every 2:00 a.m. Taco Bell run, every walk, every gaming session, every loading screen are opportunities to pray and talk to God. Think of the people we like talking to the most (even if they are NPC merchants), how often do we talk to them? God should be as often or more! The best way to start this is to make reminders for yourself, notes on the wall, stick notes on the console or controller, stickers on the laptop case, whatever way we play, whatever other activities we do can help remind us to pray often.

Just like a campaign mode consisting of multiple small missions that lead to the campaign being completed and moving on to the next campaign, a good prayer life consists of praying multiple times consistently until you have gotten into that habit then working on going deeper into your heart and life and praying for longer times after that. Just like other types of conversation though, there's never a point where you're perfect at prayer, only that you feel more comfortable praying and talking to God, whether alone or in front of others.

Chapter Questions

1. Have you ever read the entire Bible? If yes, how many times?
2. What books are the hardest for you to read? Have you tried reading them lately?
3. Reread one book, even an easy one, what new details did you notice this time?
4. How often do you pray, in crisis, weekly, daily? Has this chapter helped you develop better ideas to pray more often?
5. What's your favorite "unconventional" place to pray?

Achievement Unlocked:
ALL BY MYSELF

CHAPTER 5

Hardcore Mode

While there are two parts to solo mode, there is one thing that adds to solo mode in modern games. Usually, it's called "hardcore mode," and it makes the game more realistic in that it mirrors real life more, requiring food and sleep, making injuries hurt more, making falling more realistic in height to damage. Then there are some games that make it so hard that things give us game overs in one hit and we have to start over the entire game. If you're not Ult, you're not gonna make it in these modes. But in this case, it means the things that add to our solo mode to make our spiritual growth richer and fuller and keeps us growing rather than settling into a complacent life. In this sense, we still need to be Ult, but the consequences aren't as harrowing. We may not have explosions all around us or monsters from our deepest nightmares coming at us in waves over and over again, but these will still be really difficult for most of us to get into a habit of doing.

These things can be more difficult to get into the habit of doing regularly than getting dropped into the middle of NBA 2K20 without being told the buttons, but they are well worth the effort in the long run. And while some of them may be things you've never heard of or tried, they each add something to our lives and change us for the better if we push through any unpleasant aspects of it. Like how beating the weaker opponents in a long tournament might get tiring but the prize is only after we get through all the opponents regardless of difficulty level. And let's be honest, we can't really call ourselves gamers if we only ever play every game on the easiest difficulty setting and only get the achievements that are given as part of beating the game on easy. We need to buckle down, clear our schedule, and beast it on hardcore mode to really win. So, let's agree to put these into practice and get our spiritual life as high as our in-game stats!

While there are three aspects of hardcore mode, don't quit now, that'd be a worse betrayal of yourself than General Shepard in CoD, Atlas in Bioshock, and Wheatley in Portal combined. And since none of us want to do that level of betrayal to ourselves, we need to get deeper into God than just the basics. So, go to the settings menu, select Hardcore Mode, and start with the first aspect.

The first aspect of hardcore mode is fasting. This can definitely seem like the least fun aspect, and many of us are tempted to skip this entire part and move on to something more fun. But think about some of the hardest parts of games that are "optional" to the main story line, sometimes skipping them is easier, but the things you learn, the tricks you unlock, the bonuses that come with them, the achievements they unlock, the skills they require us to master all make the game as a whole that much better in the long run. And while some games include tedious ones that are better left undone, God isn't one of those games, and he knows what he was doing when he designed these.

So, what is fasting? Most literally, it's going without food for a time in order to focus on God, the hunger reminding us to pray and reminding us of our need for him. It's mentioned in the Bible a lot of times, and Jesus even says it's important to do as long as we're not making a big deal about our fasting and using it to make ourselves look better (Matthew 6:16–18). The time and frequency and the content of the fast changes a lot depending on factors like our health, how used to fasting we are, and our purpose.

So, how do we fast? We can start by picking something to fast that will not physically hurt us; those with low blood sugar shouldn't pick something to fast that will cause them to be ill. We also should pick something that will mean something to us because doing something like "fasting" our least favorite food is the opposite of the point, and while it may sound as good to others, we will end up no closer to God. We need to also pick what will make us think about God, so if we skip breakfast every day, then we can't "fast" breakfast. What we pick to fast also can't be something we shouldn't be doing already, such as "fasting" a sin. While it's surprising that this needs to be said, it really does need to be said nowadays. Lastly, it needs to be somewhat of a challenge, not so we can "show God how serious we are" about our time with God so he does what we want, but so we can show ourselves how serious we are about our desire to get with God so we can receive what he wants.

To give an example from video games, when we're given a quest to join a guild, we don't go and do the quests because we want to go a hundred miles out of our way and fetch some random object from the bottom of a cave. We fetch that random object to show how serious we are about joining the guild. We also can just give whatever we'd like to give because it would be more convenient, we have to give what the guild asked for specifically.

Some ideas to get started: Fast a particular meal each day for a week. Fast all meals for one day of a week if your health is good enough. Fast beverages except water if you always drink caffeine. Fast an activity you enjoy, not suggesting video games at this point, but if you need to and feel like you should, then go for it. The key is to put God and extra time with him in place of the other things, and when we are hungry or crave that specific thing, we are turning our hearts toward Jesus. If you already practice fasting regularly and want to level it up further, fast a meal and give the money, gift card, meal itself to those who are homeless or without food for that meal.

The second aspect of hardcore mode is worshipping alone. This may seem intuitive, like how we know which way to go in a football video game because it automatically points us in the right direction, but it is an important step. This isn't just listening to Christian music, though that's a good habit in and of itself because we are still putting good things in, but it's actively taking part in worship by ourselves.

So, what is worshipping alone? Taking the time to have a consistent prayer and Bible study time like we talked about before but adding a time during that to worship God. Just like in a church service, this involves music more often than not, but beyond that, it is a heart of praise even if there is no music or songs available to us.

Psalm 150 shows us what this looks like in practice: praising God in every location possible, with everything we have (instrument or not), whoever we happen to be, whoever we happen to be with, and as long as we have breath to do it.

So, how do we worship alone? Singing songs to God, even if that means in a whisper or mouthing the words if we find ourselves in a situation that louder songs would be disruptive. Praising God from our hearts and with our lives. This includes another aspect though: worshipping God by the way we live rather than just by the words we say. Our heart needs to be in it as much as our voices, and that means our lives need to match those words. So really belt it out if you're alone, and think about the words you're saying rather than your next snack run, or the achievement you're trying to unlock.

To give an example from video games: there are plenty of games where we spend the majority of time playing in co-op or team matches, but there's almost always a part of the game that is by ourselves (except games like Overwatch and Fortnite), and to really beat the game, we have to go through that solo part. The games may include music, or not, but our focus is building up our character.

Some ideas to get started: Find worship music that is enjoyable at church and listen to it when you have time to worship in a similar way privately. Set a time aside when you know you'll be alone if possible or at least more alone so you can sing. Go somewhere remote like a hiking trail where you can sing as you go. You can even find the instrumental music from games and make your own worship music by adding words to them to glorify God.

The third aspect of hardcore mode is getting health packs. Some of us never seem to need them, others of us enjoy the games but need all the health packs we can hold, whichever you personally fall under; those health packs are needed somewhere along the way. These are things that will build us up and revitalize us if we are worn down.

The first health pack is listening to sermons. Some of us feel like we do this enough on Sunday and don't need to listen to another one until the next week. Sometimes, sermons can feel as slow as playing the whole game after doing 100 speed runs in it. Sometimes, listening to a sermon's greatest challenge is not falling asleep during it, so why would it be part of hardcore mode?

It may seem obvious, but there is a lot of Bible to read and hear. One pastor on Sundays can't get through it all, even if they never deviated from it for holidays or to do a passage again. Hearing multiple sermons a week from multiple sources can help us learn, grow, and think about things we wouldn't have in our own church only once a week. And while some of us may feel our church's sermon style is not particularly exciting, there are churches all across America, and some of them are much different from whatever style we may be familiar with, and that difference can help us learn.

Getting encouragement from, and giving encouragement to, others is the second health pack. While many of us could easily think of a time where we needed encouragement, there's a lot of times we don't give the same encouragement to others. We all need to get encouragement from time to time even if we generally feel like we don't need it often. The need for encouragement, both to give and to receive, is how God made us. The lack of that encouragement coming and going shows in the many issues our society has these days. The Bible mentions encouragement over thirty times, which should show us how important it is, with one example of it being commanded of us found in 1 Thessalonians 5:11: "Therefore encourage one another and build one another up, just as you are doing."

We need to be known as encouragers. While some of us dread the idea of people coming to use with their problems, we don't have to become certified counselors to give encouragement. All we have to do is look for the little ways to encourage others in the things we see about them. Even if they are not particularly worthy of that encouragement. Think about Jesus; he was known as an encourager even with the worst hypocrites. The best thing he could say was to tell them to stop what they were doing, but he encouraged them to stop it, so there you go. I have seen many people who are less than pleasant become much more bearable from the simple act of encouraging them. And when people know we are encouragers, it changes a lot of how they interact with us.

We need to get encouragement consistently. There's something about receiving encouragement no matter what personality type we are. There's nothing better than the feeling of getting told how important you were to your team's victory in a match. That need for encouragement is built inside us, and it's something that doesn't go away. We need to seek it out if we aren't getting the encouragement we need normally. A natural question would be how we get that encouragement, and the answer is by finding a good church that cares about each member. If the church you attend isn't encouraging you consistently, there's one that's probably closer than you think that will. That's one of the reasons the Bible says being in a local church is important. As Hebrews 10:24–25 says, "Let us consider how to stir up one another to love and good works, not neglecting to meet together, as is the habit of some, but encouraging one another, and all the more as you see the day drawing near."

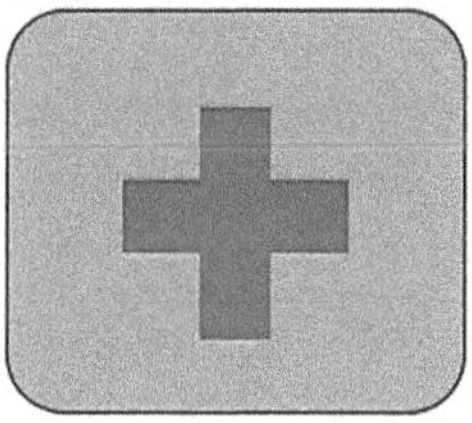

The pause button is another important health pack. We all have to pause our games from time to time. Whether it's for a run to get energy drinks, the bathroom, parents, significant others calling for something, food, work, sleep, or something else. And while many of us never think about it, we also need to pause our lives as well.

As any of us who have played older games know, those systems can overheat if played too long or not vented well enough. And we are very similar in that when we do too much too long, it begins to affect us. While many of us who have almost never hit the pause button and would currently be wondering if that's true, think about this: How often is sleep not as restful as it should be? How often is the idea of relaxing and "doing nothing" seem like it is beyond reach? Some of us hit the pause button on life inadvertently by staying home and playing games, and our body gets enough rest to endure a lot. But our soul is designed for rest as well, and our relationship with God can feel as exhausted as we do after a new game comes out and we spend three days straight playing it without realizing how little sleep we've gotten. Just like our body needs rest, we need to take time to rest from the world and focus on God.

This doesn't necessarily mean spending all day in some meditative state (which meditation is something we'll touch on later), but it does mean hitting that pause button on doing "stuff" and focusing more on God. The Bible calls it Sabbath. In the Old Testament, Israel was instructed to rest on that day and not do any work so they could worship God. And while they were commanded not to work, they were never commanded to be in a worship service all day. We are supposed to worship God in the way we live every day, but Hebrews 4:9 says, "There remains a Sabbath rest for the people of God," so we are still supposed to take a day even if it's not on Saturday, like the Jewish Sabbath, to be restful and more focused on God. A few chapters from now we'll talk more about the practicality of this, but that means we can even play video games on our "Sabbath" if our focus is still on God.

Taking a Sabbath, or "hitting the pause button," has tremendous benefits for us spiritually and practically. Taking time to rest from work gives us better time with our families and friends that can normally be just a quick meal together during the week or seeing each other before bed. This rest can also make us more productive in our work, give us time to get spiritual disciplines we've slacked on, and get a rest every week to try again for the times we fail.

There was an early mantra of older and more difficult games: "save early, save often." Anyone who has played games like KOTOR, Morrowind, or other games with either rare or no autosaves knows the value of that mantra. I personally get funny looks from those who watch me playing more modern games because of the frequency I save, due to how many times I made mistakes with my save files in games like the ones mentioned above. For the Christian life, the Sabbath is that save file. While it doesn't let us go back to before we did something like a video game save file, it does give us a time to think through the week we had, the ways we failed, the ways we succeeded, and the things we need to do differently the following week. It's a mental save file that helps us get things done right rather than rushing through.

While I cannot stress how important the Sabbath is, it's also important to remember that the Sabbath was made for us, rather than a law to feel guilty about breaking as Mark 2:23–28 reminds us. Sunday is the day many Christians pick because worship was on the Jewish Sabbath of Saturday, but the early Christians wanted to also worship on the day Jesus rose from the dead, the "first day of the week" (Acts 20:7, 1 Corinthians 16:2), and since they were already going to a local church on that day, the less Jewish believers just dropped the Saturday, but the point of the Sabbath can be applied to whatever day you set in your heart because of the way life situations can vary. So, find the day that works best for your life to make a weekly Sabbath and hit that pause button.

Solitude is the fourth health pack, and I don't mean the city in Skyrim. While many video games are played by ourselves with a screen, even there we have people we interact with and work we do. There is still a need for us to get alone with God for a longer period of time than a daily quiet time, as important as that is.

In answering the question of how we get solitude, it's important to remember the difference between being alone and being isolated. Isolated is when there is no one physically around you, and you feel that as being lonely. Isolated can be brought on us or a personal choice to avoid potential pain. And while isolation is generally negative, we do need some time alone. Being alone is just when no one else is around, and it can be very beneficial for us to focus and to give God our full attention.

As far as where we get solitude, there's a lot of variation on that answer. But the biggest thing is that you find what works with your time and your purpose. Some of us like getting into nature, and a park or trail works best. Some of us would be too distracted by that and need a quiet room. Some of us would end up beating three levels before we remembered that room was our game room and a bad choice for time with God. Some of us live with a large family, and finding a place alone is difficult, but in whatever situation we find ourselves in, it is possible. It takes some creativity at times but is well worth it. I myself have had to take a drive or wake up in the middle of the night to get that time when things were busy, but I made it work and it did change things for me.

While generally not the case, some games can even be avenues for solitude. I have had some times where a game that doesn't have anything attacking me and I wasn't achievement hunting, actually give me time with God between an audio Bible, and people thinking I'm concentrating on the game instead of having solitude, so they gave me the space I needed. Of course, I'm not giving you a license to play games and pass it off as solitude either, but that's where the personal aspect of a relationship with God comes in, and you and him need to work out what actually helps or hurts you getting time with him. I will say though, I've ignored paying the racoon for my house for hours while I used the time for God, and it's benefited me.

The final health pack is practicing meditation. By this, I don't mean "emptying your mind" and that kind of thing used in other religions and New Age movements. Meditation for Christians is actually the opposite of that. Rather than seeking to empty, it is to fill. It does mean quieting our minds but to focus them on who God is and his character and be filled with who he is.

Of course, the question is how to do that practically. And it could seem confusing or awkward at first to just "sit and think about Jesus." It's definitely one of those things that feels more natural the longer you do it, like how only in video games is it okay to walk up to a random body and pick everything off it, how we can pause a game to eat our weight in rice balls or cheese wheels, how characters can die five times and get revived but are gone forever if it's during a cutscene, or how we can beat zombies with watermelons while digging for diamonds. The first things we need to do is establish a place to practice it, and thankfully nowadays, there are a lot more places where sitting and meditating is seen as completely normal. But after sitting down and relaxing is where it really diverges because then we start to focus and think about who God is, what he has done for us, and how thankful we are for him. If that feels difficult to do for more than five minutes at first, that's okay because in our flesh, it's not natural and it's a fight. The more we practice it though, and the more we walk in the Spirit, we can see more and more of who God is and what he has done, and before long, it feel like the time flies by because we will truly be able to see how big a part of our lives he has been even behind the scenes. You can even make a list ahead of time, if need be.

There are actually several examples of this in scripture to go from. It was a common practice in the Old Testament. In Psalms, we see the largest examples, where the writers were singing from their meditations on God and made the largest book in the Bible because meditating on God is a limitless source of musical inspiration. In every example, we see the same basic ideas:

> Deeply thinking about God;
> deeply thinking about his Word;
> deeply thinking about what he has done;
> and
> deeply thinking about who he is.

Some video games can actually help with this health pack as well as much as some will be surprised by it. There are a large group of games with incredibly awesome soundtracks, like Skyrim, Breath of the Wild, and Final Fantasy, to name some. Their calming music can really help us get into a relaxed mode to think about God, provided there's no enemies nearby to make the meditation go from relaxing to jarring. There are also a lot of relaxing games that can disengage our brains enough to be able to think about God and his goodness even while we're playing, a few examples being farm games, walking games, Minecraft, and some puzzle games, like Myst and Rime.

Chapter Questions

1. What is something you need to do right now to implement these concepts?

2. Have you ever fasted before? What will you fast to practice this?
3. How often do you worship alone? What are your favorite songs?
4. Which health pack is the hardest for you to implement?
5. Which health pack is the most helpful for you? How has it helped?

Achievement Unlocked:
I THINK I SURVIVED

CHAPTER 6

Co-op Playing

While some of us play our video games to not be around others, some games require others just to get through the game, whether it's co-op modes, multiplayer modes, multiplayer achievements, bosses that are only easy enough to beat by adding the second player, MMORPGs. Many of us enjoy these kinds of social interactions much more than in the real world, and at times, I am one of those people for sure. We've all had times where the order of desired social interaction in our lives look like this:

1. Online people playing on our team
2. Online people playing the same games
3. People in real life in the video game store
4. Other interactions

But as true as that can be and as much as Christianity is a personal faith, other people are an important part of our spiritual life and growth as well. A good example of this is Dynasty Warriors 3; sure, we can get the ultimate weapons by running back and forth from our objectives to defending the leader run by an A.I. with the common sense of the NPCs with negative perception, but it's infinitely easier to have a friend/sibling be the leader of our mission so we can do objectives and they can run around not making bad choices and you can get the Sky Scorcher...except, of course, for that one time I asked my brother to be the leader and he was mad at me for something else and purposefully ran to the boss and beat the level RIGHT before I could collect the weapon! I can't believe he did that! Yes, it was my fault he got in trouble, but there's a LINE and it's WAY back there... but I digress... The point is that it's important to have other people help us with stuff...unless they're mad at you...then work that stuff out beforehand so it's not an issue.

Doing life together is important for our mental and spiritual health. This is often called fellowship in Christian circles, but if that sounds weird to use, there's a lot of other terms. Fellowship means more than just eating a meal of fried food together after church to raise money for something. It involves a deeper connection than just vaguely knowing each from church and being in the general vicinity of each other. Fellowship is a connection with others that share a heart after the same purpose. It can definitely involve food as Acts 2:42 says, "And they devoted themselves to the apostles' teaching and the fellowship, to the breaking of bread and the prayers." But real fellowship is deeper than that, it's connecting over Jesus in a way that's like when you meet someone wearing a hat or shirt from your favorite video game or when you hear someone quote an obscure line from your favorite character; there's an instant bond.

Some of us aren't fans of trying to start fellowship over Jesus, either because we've not known him long enough or don't know him as good as we should for how long we've known him and don't know what to say. But that fear that's keeping us from deeper fellowship is trying to rob us of the benefits of it, like how horror games try to keep us from moving long enough for something to be right behind us or how panic in a quick time event during a cutscene makes us instantly forget which system's controller we're using. (Why is it asking me to press triangle on Xbox! Oh, this is PlayStation...aaaannnd game over...) If that describes you, take heart, 1 Corinthians 1:9 says, "God is faithful, by whom you were called into the fellowship of his Son, Jesus Christ our Lord," which means we are literally made for fellowship because we are in Christ. It may take time to get used to the idea, but things like sharing our story of how we came to know Jesus or what we are learning from God's Word and through video games being connected to God's Word, we can have those deeper connections and fellowship.

While we already talked about Hebrews 10:24–25 in chapter 5, it's important to level up our understanding of it because it is what Fellowship is all about: "And let us consider how to stir up one another to love and good works, not neglecting to meet together, as is the habit of some, but encouraging one another, and all the more as you see the day drawing near."

Fellowship is all about how we can encourage each other to love others, which means we have to have communication with each other (but maybe with less sarcasm than we're used to). We also can't encourage each other to do good works without being around each other and either talking about the good works we did, will do, or doing those good works together. If you ever wondered why some people seem like best friends after camp or a mission trip, it's because it creates a tiny area of forced fellowship that can be the start of great continual fellowship if we remember to keep it daily (chapter 2 strikes again). And the verse sums it all up by saying that the reason we need fellowship is because Jesus is coming back and we need encouragement to be doing what we're supposed to so it isn't awkward when he comes back and sees what we're doing. Of course, he always sees what we're doing, and some of us might not make it until he comes back, but that also is part of the whole point; how embarrassing would it be for someone we want to think the world of us to see us screen watching?

Church is one of the main ways we do fellowship with other believers. And while some of us have been stuck in a church that is bad for either its approach to God or its theology, the good news for us is that church isn't one of those sports games that perfectly clone the previous game while just adding a few extra characters and adding a feature so small we never see it until we literally look into the game's code. While it may take time and giving multiple churches genuine tries, we can find a church near enough to us that promotes real fellowship and doesn't bore us to tears. Of course, the most important thing about a church is if it follows the Bible or teaches something anti-biblical, but other than that, a lot of it is preference. Some of us may, at the end of the day, have to pull a Tetris and find where we fit best even if there's no "perfect spot" available. Because after all, as the old saying goes, if a perfect church existed, we'd ruin it as soon as people came into the doors. But we can make it work if we put genuine effort into finding one. Hebrews 13:16 tells us what we need from a church at the end of the day, "Do not neglect to do good and to share what you have for such sacrifices are pleasing to God." When a church encourages us to do good, while not compromising beliefs, then the other stuff is just what we enjoy more than what we need.

Corporate worship is another important part of co-op (Psalm 102:18–22, 1 Corinthians 14:26). Just like personal worship, it goes deeper than the music. Some churches are practically a rock concert with an hour of music, but if those in the congregation are still reacting to the music like zombies just staring and listening, then there is no real worship going on, and it misses the entire point. There're also times where what some people call "good old-fashioned hymns" can be full of truth but sound as engaging as funeral music and also don't draw out worship. Corporate worship is about the people in the congregation getting involved in the worship with their words and their hearts, and as much as some people would like to argue it, we can usually feel if a church is doing this or not. All of us have off days in everything, even in worship, and whole congregations do as well, but if the church is consistently struggling to have any meaningful worship, then that's a warning sign that the corporate worship is lacking.

Personally, I have had times where the church I was attending was like the negative examples above, and it was the only church within my distance to get to. I had genuinely tried to find one that fit, but there just wasn't one. At first, I didn't know what to do, like many of you might, but I figured out who in the church DID care about worship and worshipping together, and we made a point to get together as a smaller group and worship in a way that fit our style as well as our need for genuine worship from the heart. That made a big difference for that season until I moved and could get to another church that, as a whole, made real worship a priority. Other times, I found churches in the area that were having nights of worship and went there, even if I didn't know anyone else, because everyone there was genuinely worshipping and I could feel the fellowship in that short time.

Some of us have been burned by churches before, and many never want to set foot into one again because of the negative experiences they had at places that claimed to be Bible-believing churches but practiced exactly zero biblical things. It becomes a big problem when a church treats its members wrongly and can be the opposite of the point of a church's entire purpose of love and forgiveness to help draw people to repentance (2 Corinthians 2:5–8). While sometimes a church does need to call out a member for wrong actions or wrong beliefs, it's supposed to be done in love and in gentleness to bring the person back into relationship with Jesus rather than push them away from him (Galatians 6:1–5, Ephesians 4:11–15). But some churches get so focused on the wrong things that they ignore those verses to be like the Pharisees, making extra rules to make sure they're keeping the Bible's rules.

If that situation of churches burning members describes you and has turned you off, I want you to know these three things:

- God knows what you went through, and he doesn't like it either. Even if you were dealing with a big sin in your life that a church SHOULD call out, but they called it out in the completely wrong ways, and their wrong response caused more hurts and sins when they should have shown love and forgiveness and leaving the sin for the love of Christ that calls us to turning away from sin (Romans 2:4).
- God not only knows, but he will also take care of those ministers who use the gospel for personal gain rather than to genuinely spread the gospel, and if you need more convincing of it, read Philippians 1:15–18 and James 3:1.
- God not only knows and will take care of it, but he also is wanting to be with you through it. His desire is for us to be part of the body of Christ, and that means being in the Church, the global body of believers, but also the church, the local expressions of that body together (Ephesians 4:11–16). While it may be scary and hard to try again after

> being burned, I want to encourage you to remember that you're not going alone to anywhere you try.

So that's why people hurting us shouldn't keep us from church. But that's usually not good enough to convince some of us to actually GO to church, so here are just a few of the reasons we need church, not just that the church needs us. In this day and age, it's so easy to feel alone even with tons of people on social media and on game platforms; we all need reminders that we are not alone, and church is the best place for that. While some of us have never felt more alone than at a church, good churches make sure every member is loved and knows it, so a lot of it comes down to finding a good church rather than a building to go to. Church also provides resources to grow so we can know God better and serve him in more ways. 1 Corinthians 12 uses the example of a body's many parts. Sure, we can live without certain parts, but we're designed for that to be the exception rather than the norm. Much like how we can beat some RPGs with only one-party member functioning, but it's not the best situation.

Another thing to remember is that we can't say, at the end of the day, that we love Jesus but hate his body! The church is supposed to show unbelievers who Christ is, and his love for the church is even our whole picture of what marriage should look like (Ephesians 5:25), so we can't show Christ's love for the church if we're not in it. We also can't love the lost like we're supposed to if we can't even love those who are saved. Granted at times, it's easier to love the lost because they're more honest with their stuff, but Jesus wants us to forgive like the MANY things he forgave US. Which brings us to the last part of why we need church. Church reminds us of our own need for grace because just like all those "hypocrites" who are far from perfect even though they're in church all the time, we all fall short of God's standards and are supposed to work together to acknowledge our sins and work together to get through those sins to sin less often and less intentionally than before. Because at the end of the day, we have been forgiven of much, so we must forgive much as well, and we need physical reminders of that weekly (Luke 7:36–50).

Here is another aspect about co-op mode that turns some of us off to church or being around ministries: giving. Real giving to a church is not loot crates we have to pay over and over again to beat a game. Real giving is a heart that sees how much God has given to us, and we can't help but to give back to him, his work through biblical churches, and to people in need of knowing him but also of having basic needs met. I mentioned Hebrew 13:16 a little way back, and it talks about this idea, God (and by extension a good church) encourages us to share what we have while not trying to guilt or coerce us into giving to "make God bless us" or making giving sound like a requirement for salvation because neither are true or pleasing to God.

I've been at one point, and know many others who still are, in the boat of using 2 Corinthians 9:7 as an excuse to NOT give because it says, "Each one must give as he has decided in his heart, not reluctantly or under compulsion, for God loves a cheerful giver." And many of us would say the last thing we are is cheerful when it comes to giving away money that could be used for video games and food. But that's where our walk with Christ changes as we grow. Then we start reading the verse right before 2 Corinthians 9:7 (verse 6) and see it mentions "The point is this: whoever sows sparingly will also reap sparingly, and whoever sows bountifully will also reap bountifully" and that reminds us the real reason we give cheerfully because when we see how much God has given us, we see how reasonable it is to give God more than ten percent of what he's already let us use. It's also part of growth to see that God is generous. While that doesn't mean we give a hundred percent and complain God isn't providing because we're starving, it does mean the saying is true that we "can't outgive God." When we are in a good church and see genuine needs we can help fulfill, it says more about us than about God is, we don't hold that stuff with an open hand. And the result of that cheerful giving is in verse 11 of the chapter, "You will be enriched in every way to be generous in every way, which through us will produce thanksgiving to God." So, we have a LOT of reasons to give!

For an example from my life: I have, at the time of writing, never had a job that gave me more than three thousand dollars a month. While for some of you that sounds like a lot, but for most of you, it's easy to see I'm not rolling in cash to be able to "afford" to give a lot of what I have to God. But I consistently give around fifteen percent of what I have to God, both to local churches, charities, and people in need, and I have never gone a day without food that I didn't choose to go without (granted, sometimes when I'm binge-playing, I'll miss a meal without noticing). I've gone without some gaming systems I'd enjoy and don't have a high-end gaming laptop and some games I save up for a long time to get, but God is good to me and always provides. The more generous I am, the easier it is to give with a cheerful heart!

Another aspect is playing in co-op video games. And while I don't mean just having a Christian Minecraft Server, I mean that video games with other believers can actually help our spiritual growth. And that doesn't mean that we have to spend the entire match or the entire time we're online we're talking about Jesus, but for starters, we also don't pretend we've never heard of other believers and aren't believers ourselves when we are. There should be friends we have online, even if they don't live close enough to be offline, that we look for and talk to about Jesus and what we're learning. Some examples include games that are even usually thought of as the opposite as helpful to our walk in Christ; games like Overwatch, Fortnite, Minecraft, Elder Scrolls Online, and World of Warcraft are all great examples of this opportunity to talk with others about Jesus even over our game platforms.

We also need to have people who are helping us grow and people we are helping to grow in Christ. This is normally called discipleship, but to me, that makes it sound a little official or odd sometimes. Think of it as when a character is a low level, it's great to have a guild member or a merchant to train them if the cost isn't high. And it would be a great theoretical game mechanic for it to be able to be reciprocated with followers or other NPCs. The same is true for us spiritually, we need people to challenge us, train us, and help us get better, and however bad we think we are at all this Jesus stuff, we have something to offer by the things we have learned, even if we learned a lot of what NOT to do, like don't mine at night or straight down, or we learned what to do the hard way.

And let's be honest, MOST of us learned a lot of things from what NOT to do and learned a LOT of things the hard way, so we have a lot to teach at the end of the day!

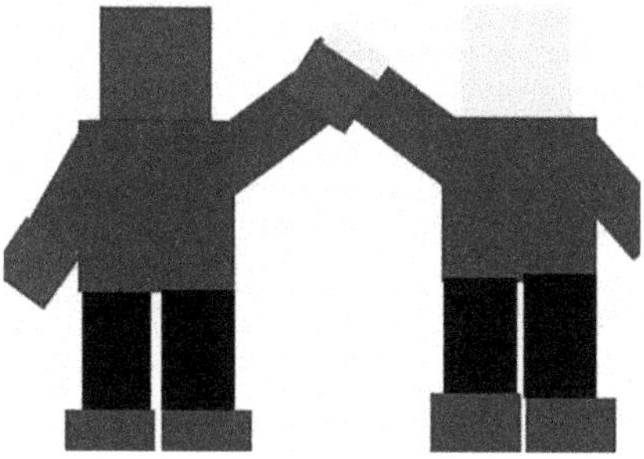

Chapter Questions

1. Do you have a regular way you fellowship? How?
2. How often do you spend quality time with friends? How much of that time is about Jesus?
3. Do you have a church you attend? How regularly?
4. Who is someone you want to teach something?
5. What's something you learned from what NOT to do?

Achievement Unlocked:
ASKING FOR A FRIEND

CHAPTER 7

Game Over?

Gamers face a few classic pitfalls, and while everyone faces these pitfalls in their lives one way or another, we face them in specific ways we can all relate to. Some of them come from the nature of video game designs, and others come from the situations within ourselves that video games have a habit of drawing out. Dealing with these alone can be more annoying than having to have a bot NPC that is essential to beat the boss but can't aim and dies in one hit from anything.

A huge thing that n00bs do is use hacks and cheats in things, like competitions and multiplayer, to get advantages because they have no skills in and of themselves. The rationale is as long as an admin doesn't catch them and ban them, it's okay, and even then, they just make a new account and do it all over again. But this attitude is something we sometimes take into our daily lives as well without even realizing it. But we're always being watched, even if no one's looking. It sounds cliché to say that Jesus is always watching, yet while we say we believe Jesus is everywhere at once, we seldom act like it when it comes to trying to get away with things we do. We need to know the truth and live like it's true. Even if we all do it, that doesn't make something right, so we need to talk about some things, lest we get into n00b territory again.

Now I have to ask you to not roll your eyes or throw the book at this point. But one pitfall gamers face is the temptation for violence.

There is a BIG misconception that video games CAUSE violence, and I'll be the most adamant defender that they do NOT cause violence. I play many video games that contain violence, and I am one of the least violent people. There are also a hoard of video games where the most violent thing we can do is hit someone with a bug net or harvest corn. I know there are a lot of gamers who enjoy games because of their story lines, or because of their realism, and the violence just happens to be there (after all, how realistic can a game be if we can shoot a bad guy with a bazooka and he just says "ouch"). None of that makes a gamer violent or enjoy violence. The entire history of the world is full of violence, even since Cain and Abel, and people have been coming up with ways to be more violent and practice violence long before the invention of video games.

Video games have only existed since 1958, with the first public game (Pong) only being in 1972, so to say that they cause violence is to ignore history up until 1972, and Pong isn't even a violent game unless someone considers tennis without people violent, so you'd have to get into more recent history for that aspect of games. Even in games with some violence in them aren't all violent, like in Oblivion when we have to let a bear attack us to show our respect for nature or using a healing spell on an enemy that is undead, dueling with a banjo instead of pistols, sitting by fires and cooking so much variety that people write entire cookbooks based on the delicious-looking game foods, or how a game goes a lot faster by just sitting there like in Far Cry 4. There's even games where there's violent options, but you barley have to do anything considered violent, and the best endings are from being as nonviolent as possible, like in Dishonored or Undertale. Anyone who wants to argue that all games are the same and games are violent need to read this part, and any of us who hear that can recommend this book to them.

The confusion sets in though because video games that HAVE a lot of violence give avenues for people who are already violent to grow in the love of violence as well as giving avenues to practice being violent. That's where things get iffy when it becomes a "training ground" for those who enjoy the violence but don't want to try it out on real people yet. Some of us started just enjoying the game because of the game itself, then enjoyed the violence in the game. After that, some of us began to look for games that have violent aspects in it for the fun of it, telling ourselves that we don't like the violence, we just like having the choices of play or the sense of realism when it's scary. Then we began to look for games that were more and more violent, and subconsciously, we get annoyed by the games that let a bad guy get wasted without gory details. This pours into our lives with actions that make people either feel like they're about to be hurt by us or are actually hurt by us when we think about the gore and violence, and it feels right instead of scary and wrong and when we can't let something we feel is a wrong go by without swift retribution. That's when it gets to be a problem we need to deal with quickly.

Why deal with it at all? Because one of the biggest things God has to deal with people about throughout history is their violence. The people of Noah's day were so violent God had to hit "reset" with only Noah's family; the people of Canaan were so violent God gave the 400 years to stop it, and when they didn't, the Israelites had to wipe them out. Israel got violent as well and had to be judged (Ezekiel 45:9), as well as Assyria, Babylon, Persia, Edom, to name just a few example of how God is not a fan of people who enjoy violence. The New Testament also talks about the dangers of violence, with Peter getting into trouble over it (Matthew 26:51–52), and multiple times in the Epistles, we're told to not be violent people (Ephesians 4:31, Colossians 3:8).

So, if we enjoy the violence of video games and look for more and more violence in games, it's time to recognize the problem. If people shrink back from us when we're talking to them because they're afraid of us, it's time to recognize the problem. Take an honest look at yourself if this may be an issue for you, and if you get into situations where you are being violent, remove yourself from that situation before you do anything violent. If it's anger-based violence, we'll talk more about that next but get away until you calm down so it doesn't manifest as violent actions. If it's a violence from enjoying the suffering of others, that needs some help beyond a book, so I encourage you to take that step and get help. But one thing I can encourage you to do from here to help is to develop more empathy. Empathy is feeling what others feel and doing something about it to make things different in a positive way. Don't just recognize someone is hurting, think of how you can personally do something to help make that suffering less rather than greater.

The next temptation is one that a majority of us can relate to: anger. Just like violence, anger is in no way caused by video games. But video games can show the underlying problem already inside us, and those who don't want to admit the underlying and preexisting problem will shift the blame onto video games or deny it exists, which is as obviously a lie than a character saying, "No, I'm NOT evil, my eyes are red and my skin is ashen white because I don't go outside much and my paramilitary soldiers bomb entire cities to promote peace!"

Of course, we all get angry sometimes, it's a natural reaction to the things going on in our lives that bring out strong emotions. The issue is how we show it that anger and how we handle that anger when we have it. Anger can be right or wrong depending on two factors:

1. why we're angry
2. how we act because of that anger

Sometimes, our anger is right and we handle it right, and that's when the anger is not only understandable but okay, like Jesus throwing the money changing tables (Matthew 21:12–13). But if we're honest, often our anger is not only for wrong reasons that shouldn't upset us as much as it does, AND we handle it wrongly as well, and that kind of anger is against what God wants for us (James 1:19–20). Some examples I'm going to use are ones that so many of us would say we've done these at least once, or some of us do them more often than we'd like to admit, but these are that happen so often they have become joke characteristics of many gamers. These are some of the very reasons that parents, grandparents, significant others, spouses, etc. think that video games cause anger and violence:

- Throwing controllers when the game follows its programming, citing the computer or another player cheating as the reason
- Screaming at strangers online for existing and accomplishing their objective
- Punching people nearby for not losing when we did

It's sad, and a little embarrassing, but it's truer than it should be. Some of us have only done one or more of those things once, or once in a blue moon when we're already stressed, but when it happens often, we need to look at the source and deal with our anger. Video games are designed to be fun and challenging, so when they make us infuriated, we need to reevaluate ourselves before we look to our games. When we realize games are bringing our anger out, we need to look for the source of that anger and confess it. We don't have to hide it or pretend it doesn't exist or get defensive when someone says our game is making us angry. In that case, we can at least confess that it's our anger that's the issue, not the game, and keep reading for some ways to help us get our anger under control so we can follow what the Bible says, "Be angry and do not sin; do not let the sun go down on your anger" (Ephesians 4:26). PS: if the sun is *already* down, that's not an excuse to stay angry, it's a metaphor for not letting your day end angry, so if it's already 3:00 a.m., don't fall asleep on the couch angry.

This next topic can be as awkward as the time they made Earthworm Jim 3D, but it's important to get into it anyway. So, please don't blush, shut the book slowly, and walk away when I say it: provocative characters in video games. Just like violence in a game, it's not a sin to recognize that characters in a game are made to appear attractive. Female and male characters are almost always designed, especially main characters and their love interests, to be the most attractive possible, and in the age of Mods and character building, it can be made even more so like that. Often those characters have less than practical armor and less than appropriate clothing in addition to their physical attributes. Of course, there's a very important thing to point out here, there's a huge difference between desire and lust, but many video games are almost designed to bring out the latter using the former as a stepping-stone.

Now some of you are going to say "Dude, I am NOT attracted to a collection of pixels!" and if you're not lying through your teeth, it still doesn't change the steps games try to take us down. While some of us aren't attracted to the characters themselves, they take us down the steps of using parts that are attractive and making us think of people the characters remind us of. So, even without the physical attraction being to the characters themselves, it can draw our thoughts to bad places. The waters get muddy because being attracted physically to anyone, even a representation of someone, is not wrong at all. Being physically attracted just means our brains are functioning as designed because God made us to be attracted to others (Song of Solomon). The problem comes in when physical attraction turns to lust, when the thoughts dwell on the attraction and go into places they aren't supposed to go and into actions that are not supposed to be done.

Some ways to distinguish between desire and lust are a few key differences. The first difference is that lust is gratifying, we say we "aren't doing anything" when someone asks what we're looking at or thinking about, and we lie to ourselves about why we're looking and where we're looking. The second difference is that it's desire, but our focus is on the "buzz" we get from looking long and hard at certain details, and it's not like desire that is redirected by focusing back onto the game itself, on our spouse if we have one, or on Jesus but goes into a thinking about the character or a person that character makes us think of. The third difference is that we enjoy it, and we lean into enjoying it rather than leaning away from it and leaning into its proper context in marriage. The fourth difference is a key determiner between desire and lust is that lust is willfully allowed, it's not like a situation we didn't expect or that is forced on us by the game's circumstances, like genuinely not knowing something was in a game did a certain thing or wears a certain thing but rather it is something we choose to do. It's taking the character's clothes off to see what they look like or putting on the most provocative clothing in the game or other such actions that are feeding lust rather than redirecting desire to its proper place. Sometimes, it is part of a bad habit we have had for a long time or we don't think about doing consciously because we let our mind wander without stopping it, but at the end, it's a choice we make. It is not forced upon us.

For example, if we were playing a game that a friend recommended to us without looking at why it's rated M+17, then proceed to see a character's clothes coming off, do we exit the game? Or even look away from it? Or do we reload the game to watch it again?

"Why is it a big deal anyway?" many will invariably ask. Closely followed by "Everyone does it!" or "It's no big deal!" or "Yeah, I'm watching it, but I don't want to miss the plot!" The reason is as simple as it gets: Jesus said NO. But that's seldom a good enough reason for most of us because we're more than a little stubborn, willful, and hardheaded. To break it down, all sin is sin because it's not good for us. More than that, lust is bad because it's adultery in Jesus's book (Matthew 5:28). We search for how we can justify our gratification of sexual desires when they are clearly wrongly directed and try to lie to ourselves and anyone who calls us out over it, and that's the evidence itself we're going the wrong way without a Koopa holding a U-Turn sign. "But I'm not even married! How can it be adultery!" many people will mentally say, sort of proving my point, but I understand the confusion.

And while there's many theories on the concept of "the one" I could use to argue that it's still adultery anyway, the best way I can think to explain it is this: You're not married until you say "I do" (or your culture's equivalent), and that's when you're married to that one person. So, anyone and anything we think about in a sexual way before that event or beyond that one person after said event is adultery, and it's something God is not a fan of believers trying to get away with (Malachi 3:5, 1 Corinthians 6:9–10, 2 Peter 2:14, Revelation 2:22).

The reason that's so bad is to use a summary of Paul in 1 Corinthians 6 because we're literally hurting ourselves, God's special creations he loves enough to die for, while at the same time telling him we're not happy with what he will/has given us in that department. We don't have what we need in that department because we aren't asking, asking the right way, or aren't listening for his answers (James 4:1–4). And while it definitely hurts a spouse and our relationship with them if we are married and acting more interested in a character than our spouse, that also is hurting us because we are one flesh even if a lot of Christians nowadays ignore the fact of marriage. Not following God's ways in this area is like choosing to permanently lose HP and get it drained continuously, and then getting confused and upset that we're getting beaten over and over.

So, the question isn't exactly "which of the sins from this chapter are particular to us?" but rather "when we sin, what do we do?"

Even if none of those three are the ones you personally struggle with, there's SOME sin you do. If any of us think we have no sin that we struggle with, that means we're into it so deep we're blind to it. Just like some of us have been blind to what level of sin we are into the above sins until now. As 1 John 1:8 put it, "If we say we have no sin, we deceive ourselves, and the truth is not in us." And just like we hate it when a character lies to us to later betray us in a game, we only hurt ourselves and hinder our progress when we lie to ourselves. And we can't complain God isn't speaking to us, leading us, guiding us, and coming through for us when we're regularly telling him to stop talking to us or ignore us while we sin. Consider this a spiritual equivalent to a racing game's "wrong way" drop-down warning. Since we will sin, there's things we need to do rather than let ourselves stay down. Now's the time to admit it, turn around, and find out what to do from here.

The first thing to do is the most obvious when we royally mess up a game or get a game over: reload our save file!

Proverbs 24:16 puts it this way: "For the righteous falls seven times and rises again but the wicked stumble in times of calamity." We have a choice when we sin, and especially when it's a sin that becomes a habit, to be wicked and fall into calamity, or be the righteous person who we really are in Christ. While after admitting to ourselves the sins we do, we may not feel like we are righteous, but we need to remember chapter 1 and how we are righteous because of Jesus rather than because of what we have or haven't done. So, in those moments, we need to be honest with our sin, and we need to reload and restart our file.

While we can't go back to the literal point before we sinned, we have God's version of autosave: "If we confess our sins, he is faithful and just to forgive us our sins and to cleanse us from all unrighteousness" (1 John 1:9). It all starts with the truth, we sinned and we need to confess it. We don't deny it is sin or make excuses but ask for forgiveness for the sins we know about (our sins) and for the ones we've done without realizing we did it (all unrighteousness). I've had to apply this more times than I'd like to admit, but I'm equally thankful it's true!

We don't stop at confessing our sins to God though because otherwise it creates a cycle of sinning and confession that will only draw us further from God each time and make us more prone to sin by saying something along the lines of "Well, I'm really wanting to sin right now, and it's okay if I do it this one time because I'll just confess it." We need to do some things to it out of being a habit. Because 1 John 3:6–8 remind us: "No one who abides in him keeps on sinning; no one who keeps on sinning has either seen him or known him. Little children, let no one deceive you. Whoever practices righteousness is righteous as he is righteous. Whoever makes a practice of sinning is of the devil, for the devil has been sinning from the beginning. The reason the Son of God appeared was to destroy the works of the devil."

We also need to not fail the same way over and over again. When we do happen to sin, we need to fail forward. Rather than looking back at the sins we did, we need to look forward to how we can do things differently and do better. The second thing is to renew our mind as Romans 12:2 says, "Do not be conformed to this world but be transformed by the renewal of your mind, that by testing you may discern what is the will of God, what is good and acceptable and perfect."

We can't keep thinking the same way and expect to get out of a specific habit, just like how it makes no sense how Dr. Wily throws basically the same group of single-powered bad guys at Mega Man expecting to win rather than fighting Mega Man with every one of their powers at once. We need to change how we think and feel about it and let that change what we do to expect to get different results and get rid of those things we shouldn't be doing for good (James 1:21).

We need some strategies for overcoming sins rather than just a simple idea that "sin is bad" and we should "stop it." Just like when we can't figure out a puzzle or how to beat a boss, we can sometimes need a strategy guide. Because dealing with sin on our own is harder than playing Star Fox Zero with motion controls.

Let's be clear about one point: we cannot shut down our desires and thoughts, nor should we seek to. They are not the real problem. We must also recognize and repent whenever we misuse our desires or thoughts to accommodate sin and to develop practical strategies for gaining victory if we find ourselves being dominated by this sin. However, our desires and thoughts do not force us to sin. Instead of slipping into sin, we need to act with the knowledge and confidence that God is faithful to provide "the way of escape" (1 Corinthians 10:13) whenever we are tempted.

One strategy is to remember "the cake is a lie." Sin is tempting to do because it is "fun," but the "benefits" of it are temporary at best (Hebrews 11:25) and always costs more than it's worth at the end of the day (Romans 6:23, 1 John 5:16–18). The pleasures of temptation are very temporary, and just like the cake, they lie about being worth it. We usually are good at coming up with reasons to give into sin; what we need practice in is looking for the reasons to not give in. We need to realize the temptations are there before we give into them and sin. And the times we fail, we need to confess and turn. There will always be "good reasons" to sin in the moment, and we may feel like we can't come up with any good reasons not to sin at the time, but 2 Corinthians 10:5 reminds us that we can take every thought captive and put it under Jesus's feet so they can't stay over our heads. Many of the temptations we face just need to be faced with an attitude of resistance rather than an attitude of defeat, and we will see them give way (James 4:7). The five-second rule is not just for food, put it into practice with giving into temptations as well: take five seconds to think about it before just jumping into it and give Jesus room to help say no.

Another strategy is to walk in Spirit. This sounds hyper-spiritual, and some people talk about it like it's some weird thing they can't do (and sometimes like some weird thing they do but we certainly can't). Galatians 5 though is where we get this idea, and the things Paul is telling the people to do there aren't hyper-spiritual, nor was he writing to super-Christians who can do awesome spiritual things we can't hope to do. The things we need to do to walk in the Spirit are already ours in Christ, they aren't things we earn or unlock or "try harder to do" because walking in him is our source of life in the first place (Romans 8:13). We need to look for healthy and correct outlets for lust, anger, and violence, not venting or "getting it out of our system" but redirecting our feelings into things that will honor God and building up ourselves and others instead of tearing down. For example: being short-tempered is never an admirable trait, but we tolerate it in ourselves far more than we should. And we need to build up our temper and lengthen our fuse instead of letting it be short. Galatians 5 says it in the fruit of the Spirit as "patience," and Proverbs 16:32 says it as "Whoever is slow to anger is better than the mighty, and he who rules his spirit than he who takes a city." So, as we work to build up that temper to be less angry or violent, we actually get stronger than some of our favorite and most powerful characters.

A strategy that those who enjoy Zelda games are very familiar with is to watch out for blood moons. We all have seasons, times of day, situations where we feel temptation stronger, when our enemy feels stronger, and we feel like we are less effective at resisting. An important strategy is noticing when those times are and doing things to shore up your defenses. Like how when a blood moon is rising, it's much less smart to beat a bunch of hard bad guys because they'll come back in just a second. We don't walk into the floor traps we know are there, nor do we passively accept it when our NPC follower does the same thing, so we can't do it in our spiritual lives either. We have to look for patterns of stress, exhaustion, boredom, other feelings that cause us to stumble. Watch out when we know we're tired or stressed and plan accordingly. Call friends, read the Bible, get around people, take a nap, get outside, put on worship music (or even Christian rock or rap if it helps), do whatever is needed to win rather than get beat when the health bar is obviously low, even pause and eat sixty-five wheels of cheese! (That last one is a joke, please, do not eat that much cheese, it is NOT as helpful as in games…I *may* have tried that once…) Whatever we do, we can't make excuses about our sin. We aren't some n00b who blames our loss on servers, screen watchers, bad teammates, glitches, and lots of other poor excuses.

If it's still hard, then this next strategy may help. Like any game that's just plain too hard for us at first, we have to set the difficulty to "easy." We need to do stuff to set the difficulty down to a more manageable level. We can get friends and family who can help us in times of temptation or let them call to check on us or come up with incentives to help manage our struggles while we're working on it, like how an ally helps us learn to do a barrel roll. One example is I had a friend I would put money toward a new game he wanted if he could go for a month without throwing the controller or yelling at people, and it helped him remember to lengthen his temper while he was working on it. Other times we need to go to the Bible and do something really practical. When Joseph was being tempted by Potiphar's wife in Genesis 39, he didn't just tell himself "Don't do anything with her." When she got close to him and was trying to seduce him, he just ran like something from Dark Souls, Resident Evil, Silent Hill, and Dead Space combined was chasing him. Sometimes, we gotta just RUN, physically getting away from the temptation as fast as possible without worrying about looking odd.

*Disclaimer: PLEASE, don't throw your handheld system or controller away from you if you do run, set it down before you begin running, they are expensive, and I don't want to hear about being responsible for it because it was my suggestion.

At the end of the day, we do need to take an honest look at our games when we are struggling. Are they bringing out our anger, violence, or lust? We may need to pause some of the games (especially the grittier games we may enjoy but are honestly not good for us) until we can deal with the roots of the problems and figure out how to play them without the temptations they lead us to. And if we're honest, it might mean selling the game or deleting the file to not play them anymore if we can't get away. For example, when we realize games are bringing our anger out, we need to try games that will make us less angry until we can control our temper better. Sometimes, this means pausing some of our favorite games while we work on it, but the short time away from those games, combined with the vast quantity of games that may help better, makes the work worth it for the results.

It is important to really look at our games if they happen to be grittier or have more questionable content in them. This is a very sensitive topic for many gamers, but we have to be honest with them and if they actually are negatively affecting us. Some of these sins we struggle with are like boss fights, and we can only either beat the boss and move on in the game or keep starting over right before the cutscene introducing the boss and do it all over again. Since that only leads to frustration, we need to be sure our games aren't causing those sins to add to that frustration. It's something where only you can decide if God is telling you to change, but if God is telling you to change some of those game habits, only you can decide if you will listen to him as well. This change might feel radical, but if we read through Acts 19, we can see when believers make that choice to follow God no matter the cost. "The word of the Lord continued to increase and prevail mightily" (verse 20).

When it gets hard, and it will when we're actually fighting our temptations instead of just giving into them as soon as we have them, we need to remember our Savior. Not in the way some present him, glaring at us while we sin or glaring at us because we sinned, but as the one who died on the cross to forgive that sin and wants what's best for us to help us keep from sinning and wants what's best for us even if we win. A great example of this song is a rhyme some of us have heard since infancy while others may have never heard it before:

> Oh, be careful little eyes what you see,
> Oh, be careful little eyes what you see,
> For the Father up above is looking down in love,
> Oh, be careful little eyes what you see.

The key there is *looking down in love*, not looking down in anger or in hate or in disappointment. I already mentioned this before, but it's worth going over again: it's his kindness that leads us to change, and we need to remember that when working through these sins (Romans 2:4). So, even when we fail and fall into temptation, we can't stay in sin because he is looking down in love for us to come back to him and try again.

Next chapter looks at some practical ways to beat the real boss, who, in addition to our own bad choices, is behind our temptations and struggles.

Chapter Questions

1. Which sins are the ones you specifically struggle with?
2. How long have you been actively fighting them?
3. What tips are you going to put into practice now?
4. What ways are you going to get help to deal with them?
5. How did this chapter help you see the ways the battle is winnable?

Achievement Unlocked:
LOADING SAVE FILE...

CHAPTER 8

Beating the Boss

Almost every game has a boss, some have multiple bosses, some have bad guys who we think is *the* boss only for them to have been a half-way boss, some have a surprise boss, and some have a boss who we spend hours and game over after game over beating only for their health bar to simply change color or the music to get even more intense. We need to know who the real boss is in our spiritual lives, and we need to know how to beat the boss so we don't get game over after game over in real life until we get so mad we quit and just go in-game fishing instead of worrying about it.

We shouldn't let ourselves be the boss who turns out not to be the boss. We need to get out of our own way rather than be the thing holding our walk back. If we work on the sins that trip us up and resist instead of giving in, we will go a long way toward reaching the actual boss of the game. It also helps if we don't look for ways to sin and just simply "not get caught" because, again, it's true that God is omniscient, and just like the Dark Brotherhood in Oblivion, he knows.

So, what is the real boss's identity?

Satan. Or to be more specific, the fallen angels are the real enemies, with Satan being the real boss. And while that may get some eye rolls, Jesus talks about Satan as a real being, not some concept or fairy tale, and he would know, being there when Satan got kicked out of heaven and seeing him make a mess on earth and literally being on earth to fix the results of that (Luke 10:18).

While Satan is real, there is a lot of confusion about what he's like. The Bible calls us not to be ignorant of him and what he does (2 Corinthians 2:10–11), so we need to look into what's true and not true about him. He is not all-powerful like God is because he will lose, and that's guaranteed (Romans 16:20). He is not all-knowing like God, which is why he relies on demons to feed him information (Ephesians 6:12). He is also not all-present like God is and can't be the one causing all our problems but relies on his minions to do the tempting and problem causing for us. Satan is a created being, and while he has some power over the world for now (2 Corinthians 4:4), it is only for a time. And while he does have a lot of abilities (Job 1:6, 1 Chronicles 21:1, Zechariah 3:1, Acts 26:18), like every bad guy in the games, he is going to lose (Revelation 20–22).

Satan is like a roaring lion, looking to take us down (1 Peter 5:8), he can only say lies so it's not smart to listen to him (John 8:44), is our opponent fighting against us even if we're not trying to fight him (1 Timothy 5:14, 1 Peter 5:8), and is a deceiver trying to trick us into messing up and not winning like we are meant to (Revelation 12:9). Him and his minions are not even that hard to defeat according to Scripture, all we have to do is actively resist Satan and he will flee from us (James 4:7). One of the main reasons that Jesus even came to earth, other than to save us from sin, was to signal the beginning of the end of Satan's power as he says, "The reason the Son of God appeared was to destroy the works of the devil" (1 John 3:8). So, we not only have to power to make him flee but also have the ultimate companion who is crushing the boss, much like Raiden getting his sword and beating Armstrong in Metal Gear Rising: Revengeance.

This is important to know because a lot of people we think are the main enemy in a game turn out to be wrong, and real life is like that too. For example, people are never our real enemies, Satan is the real villain, and demons are the bad guys under him. And while some people think of Satan as ruling hell, it was made for him to be in suffering as well (Revelation 20:10). And while he does control demons, and while they can possess nonbelievers at times and oppress believers, people are never the real bad guys in life. Ephesians 6:12 puts it this way: "For we do not wrestle against flesh and blood but against the rulers, against the authorities, against the cosmic powers over this present darkness, against the spiritual forces of evil in the heavenly places."

When we have problems with other people, they are never the source of the issue. That's one of the reasons yelling at people over the internet is less than helpful to them and ourselves. (Spoilers for Bioshock and Knights of the Old Republic in the next sentence.) When we look for a physical source to a spiritual problem, it's like trying to beat Andrew Ryan when Atlas is the real problem or looking for Darth Malak and trying to stop him when the player is his master the entire time. It seems right and feels like what we're supposed to do, but in the end, it just sets us up for a reveal of who the real problem is. Which is one of the reasons Romans 12:17–21 says, "Repay no one evil for evil but give thought to do what is honorable in the sight of all. If possible, so far as it depends on you, live peaceably with all. Beloved, never avenge yourselves, but leave it to the wrath of God, for it is written, 'Vengeance is mine, I will repay, says the Lord.' To the contrary, 'if your enemy is hungry, feed him; if he is thirsty, give him something to drink; for by so doing you will heap burning coals on his head.' Do not be overcome by evil, but overcome evil with good."

While it's important to know who the real boss is, it is also important to not underestimate him. Acts 19:11–16 tells a story of a group trying to cast out demons. The group are not Christians but had seen the success of Paul using the name of Jesus to get rid of the demons, and they thought they'd try the same method. They end up getting the demon's attention, but because the demon knows Jesus and his authority over demons and knows of Paul but has no idea who the people in the group was because they are not in Christ to have his protection, the demon ends up beating them up, and one demon-possessed person beats all seven men in the group and makes them run out of the house naked. All in all, a bad day for the group.

Just like how knowing a theory on beating the boss or having a player's guide doesn't mean it's easy to actually do it, knowing about Satan and demons and who they are doesn't mean we should be arrogant in handling them or trying to seek them out. One of the things the New Testament, in addition to an even larger number of times in the Old Testament, consistently warns believers to avoid is the occult, not because it's something cool and the Bible is trying to kill our fun, but because it's never a good idea to open ourselves up to the enemy's attacks (Galatians 5:19–21, Colossians 2:18, 1 John 4:1:3, 5:18–19, Revelation 21:8, 22:15). Just like how we wouldn't want to just give someone behind us a blue shell to wreck us and take us from first place to sixth place and how we don't want to help the evil organization to take over the world and how we'd rather not turn the corner to a grenade right before we get our best streak ever.

The boss's identity means that we shouldn't underestimate him or dabble in demonic things but at the same time we don't need to fear the boss or his minions. Because 1 John 4:4 literally says, "You are from God and have overcome them, for he who is in you is greater than he who is in the world." We are stronger not because of who we are but because the one inside us. That's why we don't play with things like that but also why we can boldly fight against them. Our character may have horrible stats alone, but we have invincibility and unlimited ammo, no reloads unlocked, so nothing the enemy does can hurt us unless we try to be allies (which would end worse than when Kerrigan and Raynor allied with the Sons of Korhal in StarCraft).

So, in order to not lose, and win the victory, all we need to do is stand in Christ. To stand well though, we need to equip ourselves with God's armor and remain strong in the face of the evil plans the boss has for us as individuals, us as the Body of Christ, and us as humans. This armor is listed in Ephesians 6:10–20.

Those verses read like this:

> We have the ability to stand strong in God's might (which is infinite) if we have his armor on, which is as invulnerable as he is if we're wearing it properly. Since our fight is spiritual, that means our armor is also spiritual, which I personally wish it was visible armor because that would make it a lot easier to put on and a lot cooler looking to see

> us walking around in full armor, but God gives us the best way, not the easiest way or the way we feel would be coolest.

First, we have a belt of truth because that's what keeps us centered. It also holds some of the other pieces in place and keeps us from ending up with our pants around our ankles and tripping on our face. It also anchors our sword to us, which we can all agree is essential to winning a fight. This piece is important because God is truth, so we need the truth in us to beat Satan, who is the father of lies (John 8:44).

Then we have a breastplate of righteousness because God's righteousness protects our hearts from getting destroyed by the stuff life throws at us. Like any good breastplate, living in the righteousness we have in Christ protects us as we assault the enemy. It has no back like a cuirass, but that's because we are made to not retreat, and if we are surrounded, we are made to have others help us and guard our backs (Galatians 6:2, Ephesians 4:16, Philippians 2:4).

Then we have the Roman equivalent to cleats to keep us in place when getting pushed back, and so we can advance through any terrain. Those shoes are the Gospel of Peace because we are meant to push forward and not retreat while fighting the spiritual enemies. The way we advance is the Gospel of Peace, as any study of Church history shows we only advance by preaching the Gospel, and showing it in love and peace. When we ignore the gospel, or we try to advance the gospel by violent means, that's when unbelievers stop listening and the church shrinks. Even when we are being killed for our faith, as long as we are advancing with the Gospel of Peace, the Body of Christ expands.

Then we have a shield of faith because Satan and his minions are hurling fire darts at us. Without faith in God, and being sure he's protecting us, we'd get pinned like Festus Krex in Skyrim. Faith is not just guessing or wishing God is real and what we believe is true, faith is being sure of what we believe even if we can't see it (Hebrews 11:1–3). Faith isn't a guess or a blind jump, it's seeing God's truth, his love, the facts, and knowing all that means the rest of it is true as well. Like how scientists knew of atoms before they could see them from the evidence, they had or how we know we'll win the game even when our party looks like it can't ever get out of the mess it's in and the boss seems unbeatable. God can't NOT come through for us, so it only makes sense to have faith in what he says about us and the things he tells us to do.

Then there's the helmet of salvation because we need the mental reminders of our position in Christ to keep our mind from going to the wrong places. Just like getting button combinations right or being able to have the right timing in a game, our salvation is won or lost in the mind. We are saved by grace only (Ephesians 2:8), but as long as our mind isn't protected in that salvation and we are thrown around mentally by our sin patterns and doubts of our salvation, we will never be at a place where we can win over the enemy (Ephesians 4:14).

And the last piece is our offensive weapon: the sword of the Spirit, God's Word. Like the other pieces, while it would be awesome to see it, it is stronger because it is a spiritual weapon and our real enemies are spiritual as 2 Corinthians 10:3–4 tells us, "For though we walk in the flesh, we are not waging war according to the flesh. For the weapons of our warfare are not of the flesh but have divine power to destroy strongholds." We can take down spiritual fortresses because our weapons are powered by the infinite and all-powerful God of the universe! Hebrews 4:12 even calls it sharper than the sharpest sword, so if video games have taught us anything, that means that it can cut a spiritual enemy in half before they even realize we've swung it and they'll fall in half while we dramatically walk away.

Talk about something being OP in the best way! Only this OP weapon isn't one we never end up using because the ammo is so limited because we have unlimited ammo! (For those of you non-gamers who happened to have made it this far, OP means "overpowered.") It's something the Doom Slayer wishes he had! The Word of God is not only unlimited in things we can find in it, but it's also unlimited in that we have hard copies, apps, audio Bibles, Bible movies, plays, and every other form of media imaginable that we can get the Bible into our hearts and minds to make it always on hand. It's like a weapon that we can only not have to fight the enemy if we decide to put it down and ignore it so we can let the enemy whale on us and jump into sin rather than use it to resist and fight.

God's Word is a weapon because it's all we need to defeat the enemy and win the battle, and while sometimes people look at it as a boring old book, that's just what the enemy wants. It's like a quest item we can accidentally sell, only to realize too late we really need it and have to go hunt it down and waste a lot of time doing what we should have had all along. There have been many times in my life where it would have been really great to have remembered the Bible better in order to fix a spiritual problem, and then I had to look high and low through the Bible to find that answer instead of just putting the Bible in my heart and mind in the first place so I could find it easier, and the more I've gotten into it, the easier it is to solve those issues. And while many people lately look at the Bible like just another book with myths and moral lessons, it's powerful when it comes to the spiritual war we have going on. Even some devout atheists like Lee Strobel and Josh McDowell became believers after examining it, and the spiritual enemies are just as scared of the power of God that comes through its truth (James 2:19).

At the end of the day, even if the battle feels hard to win against sin, temptation, and Satan, we can also be confident that they are going to lose the war. Even if we lose a battle once in a while, or if we lose battles often, however strong Satan is or how persuasive those who follow him are, God is much stronger and has the final say and the final win (2 Peter 2:1–4). Even when we feel like we're doing nothing but losing, God keeps us in him and makes us holy because of who he is and the source of our holiness in the first place (John 10:28, 2 Timothy 2:10–13). Like an awesome game that has an ending someone happened to have spoiled, we don't have to worry about how it will all turn out. The meantime is just subplots we have to figure out. And even those subplots are things we don't have to worry about so much as walk in and get out of our own way.

As bad, scary, interesting, or any other adjective we can use to describe our enemy, we don't need to have the feeling of dread that comes with being in the middle of nowhere with nothing around and then the game autosaves and the music changes. All we need to do is focus on the one who is our victory: Jesus (Colossians 3:1–4). The more we look to Jesus, the less the battle bothers us. Jude puts it this way, we don't need to think about demons or Satan or "rebuke them" as some circles do with good intentions. This is because God is the only one we need to be thinking about, and he is the one who will rebuke Satan when we need it (Jude 8–10). We have authority in Christ to get rid of demons from possessing or oppressing people, but the rebuking and judgment belongs to God.

If all this seems hard, and it's still difficult to get through the lies and temptations of the enemy, then use a trick we know all too well in games where the bad guys all of a sudden get harder than our character's level can handle or what we do when we KNOW the boss is going to be ridiculously difficult for us to beat...

Grind Levels

What does that look like for our spiritual lives?

We can take time to be with Jesus for long periods of time. We can get into his word in two ways: we read the Bible as a whole a lot in a short time, and we read the Bible by the topics and stories to get the overall views of the Bible. I mentioned these in "Solo Mode," but if we're reading this book straight through, there isn't always time to put it all into practice, and, of course, there's always the chance some of us have been reading it so slowly we forgot that part already. So, we get into his Word so his Word gets into us. When we do this, it builds up our faith and resistance to sins and the tools of the devil.

We can also look for resources on specific areas we'd like to grow in. While this book is one type of resource, it's not all encompassing, so we can look for other works or articles on topics we'd like more details on. This can help if we need more specific tips on getting rid of specific sins or link us to others who can help us with problems that take longer to deal with. Especially if there is no one around who can help us with problems that won't go away without working through them, like some types of violence and anger are best dealt with by a

Christian counselor. They can help work through issues and provide accountability that will help us grow by leaps and bounds by helping our thoughts and patterns change while being rooted in Christ.

Don't forget to try applying the other truths from Solo Mode and Hardcore Mode more directly, if they haven't been applied yet, and more consistently if they have been applied already. This also is a way to grind levels, by applying resources like this one rather than just reading it, thinking "that was cool" and then going back to our games. Because knowing a lot of stuff doesn't help our walk with Christ, only applying it does (James 1:22).

All this is our level grinding that can help us get rid of the sins that trip us up and help us to look at Jesus to be able to beat the boss like we were made to! Just like Hebrews 12:1 says, "Therefore, since we are surrounded by so great a cloud of witnesses, let us also lay aside every weight and sin which clings so closely, and let us run with endurance the race that is set before us."

While these won't make life as easy as finding the one spot, like a rock or piece of metal in a boss battle that the boss just can't hit us (looking at *you guys,* Thresher Maw and Warrior), they will help us know how to fight and remember that we are fighting from a place of victory rather than trying to win the victory. That's why it is so vital that we are sure we know Jesus. Because doing God's will and God's way without a relationship with him isn't God's way at all.

Chapter Questions

1. What is one thing about the boss's identity that was new for you?
2. Do you feel more scared, confident, or curious about the enemy?
3. How often do you confuse people for the real enemy?
4. How familiar are you with our armor and weapons?
5. How many levels do you feel like you need to grind?

Achievement Unlocked:
DANTE WOULD BE PROUD

CHAPTER 9

Easter Eggs

In every good game, there are what we call "Easter Eggs," and for the non-gamer who somehow bought this book and has read this far, those are not a reference to actual Easter eggs but rather are little nods within a game to outside material. It may be to other video games from the same developer, to different games entirely, to jokes about games in general, or to people outside video games. They are fun little details that sometimes are confusing without knowing the reference and sometimes are just plain awesome. Sometimes, finding an Easter egg itself is as fun as parts of the actual game, and they mark attention to detail within a game.

God made the first Easter eggs himself. Like other good things, we are just kind of using his idea. This is a big statement, which certainly needs to be shown, but rest assured that it's true! Any casual reading of the Bible shows God references things in the past to remind our thick skulls that he is just as faithful now as he was then. That's a direct reference, but what about something we could truly call as Easter eggs? Well, that is revealed in Romans 1:18–20:

> For the wrath of God is revealed from heaven against all ungodliness and unrighteousness of men, who by their unrighteousness suppress the truth. For what can be known about God is plain to them because God has shown it to them. For his invisible attributes, namely, his eternal power

> and divine nature, have been clearly perceived ever since the creation of the world, in the things that have been made. So, they are without excuse.

The reason God doesn't let anyone off the hook about knowing him and following him is because the universe is full of Easter eggs. The first one is his eternal power, which is both his ability to do anything and his always being here forever both directions. Looking at the universe should easily remind us that God has always been here because nothing else could explain the creation of something that seems infinite the further we go out *and* the further we go in, all from nothing, without a someone who was always here to make the "nothing," the "something" came from, and only he is powerful enough to create everything without anything but himself to go off. The second one is his divine nature, which is his uniqueness and godhood. Looking at the universe should make it obvious that there's only one God who could be responsible for it because the multiple deities in every culture with them makes them look too unstable for the universe to function without being destroyed by crazy deity wars.

Just like in a video game, these Easter eggs from God are not always right in front of our faces. It takes time and practice, but the more we look, the more we can find God in the details. These little details we can see him in are his Easter eggs, and usually they are only seen through hindsight, like the achievements we have to do another run through because we never knew they existed on our first play. It's watching what has happened in our lives and seeing what little moments made big differences to put us where we are now and how he has prepared us for what he wants us to do. If someone told me playing video games would help me become an author, I probably would have laughed, but here I am, with this book in your hand or on your e-reader. I also would never have guessed I would be a missionary in Thailand or a teacher in America, but God fit things together in very specific ways.

One example of this in Scripture is the entire book of Esther. God isn't mentioned by name in it, but the entire book shows how God works behind the scenes to save the day. Like a character who does all the work and somehow still isn't seen as the most important person in the in-game world for some reason (I saved everyone and all I get is some armor that isn't as good as what I'm wearing right now?). Not being mentioned doesn't do anything to hide the fact that God is the central figure and the one who saved the day. This can be seen by Esther telling Mordecai to fast in 4:16, which is going without food to pray and show how serious we are about our prayers to ourselves and God as we already talked about before. God answers by using Esther to save the day, like the times we help someone save the day and do the big part of the work only for them to get the main credit. But the feast day of Purim that follows shows God and his people win.

He also makes Easter eggs in very different places. Like when someone asks if we like PC, Xbox, PlayStation, or Nintendo and we say "yes," God doesn't have to choose if the way he will show himself is obvious ways or in subtle ways. There have been many recorded times, both in Scripture and in history, that God moves in the really big ways: the Walls of Jericho, Daniel in the Lion's Den, Jesus... doing anything, Paul raising the dead, persecuted Christians being so courageous their persecutors join them, people getting healed when the doctors say there is nothing more they can do. But there have been equally, or arguably more, times when God moves in the subtle ways we can hardly see until much later; the still, small voice in 1 Kings 19, little faith moving mountains (Matthew 17:20), being faithful with our little leading to bigger responsibilities (Luke 16:10), five loaves and two fish feeding thousands (John 6:1–14). God does the same things in our lives, and if we haven't been seeing the little and big ways, he moves then he wants to show us those!

He even makes Easter eggs in the most unlikely of places. The Bible makes it clear there is only one way to heaven, which we discussed in the beginning of the book being faith in God by Jesus and Jesus is the only way (John 14:6), but that doesn't mean that God hasn't hidden truths in other religions that we can use as bridges to the gospel to connect the wrong things people believe with some aspects of truth in them to the truth that can save them. It all goes back to the fall (Genesis 3) and the Tower of Babel (Genesis 11). We started out knowing God, and knowing the truth, but as languages split from our own mistakes, things changed. Romans 1:21–25 gives the commentary of what happened:

> For although they knew God, they did not honor him as God or give thanks to him, but they became futile in their thinking, and their foolish hearts were darkened. Claiming to be wise, they became fools and exchanged the glory of the immortal God for images resembling mortal man and birds and animals and creeping things. Therefore, God gave them up in the lusts of their hearts to impurity, to the dishonoring of their bodies among themselves, because they exchanged the truth about God for a lie and worshipped and served the creature rather than the Creator, who is blessed forever! Amen.

We started out right and then changed truth for the things created, and ever since then, we've had a hard time seeing the difference between the truth of God and the twisted truths that are remnants of where the people knowing the truth broke from it. But for us, that means we can seek those parts that are true and use them as bridges to the gospel and the truth. One example is that Buddhism teaches that we can do good deeds to "make merit," and that merit, or the lack thereof because of bad deeds, decides our next life. While the Bible says we are judged in the one and only next life by our good and bad works, none of us can make enough merit to earn heaven because of our bad deeds far outweighing our good. But then another part of Buddhism comes in, the concept that we can earn merit for others. We can never do enough to make up for the bad things we've done, let alone do it enough for others, BUT Jesus was perfect, and his perfection is enough for all who have faith in him to be counted as righteous because of his righteousness (2 Corinthians 5:21).

We can also see Easter eggs in things that seemingly have nothing to do with God. Even little things in video games can connect to truths about God. Of course, this goes back to much earlier chapters in this: we need to be getting the truth into us from God's Word for us to be able to connect video games to that truth. Like a game without any code won't play, our minds without the truth in us can't connect things to the truth. But just getting the Word in us isn't enough to see these Easter eggs in our video games, or a lot of people who are against video games would be for them. I've even seen entire articles arguing against Christians playing video games, using "'All things are lawful,' but not all things are helpful. 'All things are lawful,' but not all things build up," saying that video games are "not helpful" and "don't build up."

I hope you've seen by now my theology is a *little* different from that.

While those who don't see God's Easter eggs might think the above verse and deduction from said verse is good reasoning, I'm going to help show some ways that I personally connect everything I do, even in video games, to the truth, so even with video games, I can emulate 1 Corinthians 10:31, which I mentioned in chapter 3, but not we're going to level it up by looking more at it. "So, whether you eat or drink, or whatever you do, do all to the glory of God." And while we can't *sin* for the glory of God, video games are not sin, so they can be done for the glory of God, *if* we let them be. So, when I play games and I look for these Easter eggs through the eyes of 1 Corinthians 10:31, I find plenty of things that are echoes of God and bridges to the gospel. Like how Jesus used everyday illustrations to share parables, our video games can be those everyday link to God and his truth.

"Whatever you do" obviously includes video games, so here's the *how*.

The first Easter egg example is the Koroks in Breath of the Wild. Koroks are hidden throughout the world, and finding them is sometimes really easy, other times it takes a lot of looking to find them. But the thing is, when we look for God, it may seem hard at first, and finding God in every single place he is in our lives is really difficult because he is in the obvious and the hidden things, but there's nine hundred places he is in, so it's easy to find him *somewhere*. Unlike Koroks though, there's infinite benefits to seeing him and finding where he is in our lives, instead of an odd trophy.

Video games can be Easter eggs themselves because they help us to picture things, even within the Bible and things about God. Think about this: how many games do we get to build a house for ourselves? This really helps us picture 1 Corinthians 3:12–16 when the Bible says, "Now if anyone builds on the foundation with gold, silver, precious stones, wood, hay, straw, each one's work will become manifest, for the day will disclose it, because it will be revealed by fire, and the fire will test what sort of work each one has done. If the work that anyone has built on the foundation survives, he will receive a reward. If anyone's work is burned up, he will suffer loss, though he himself will be saved, but only as through fire. Do you not know that you are God's temple and that God's Spirit dwells in you?"

We can also mentally picture visuals better than those who haven't played games or studied biblical cultures with things like the armor of God because we see so much ancient armor in games, and we understand weapons of spiritual warfare because we use so many varieties of weapons in our games. We have to be careful with this, of course, because we all know some games stretch the "based on true events" idea, and many games picture places like hell but in ways that don't line up with the Bible, but they still help us picture situations like the battle of Armageddon in Revelation 16 and the new heaven and earth in Revelation 21 because of the unworldly places we've been to through our video games and how our imagination has been enhanced by them.

Another example seems like it's a stretch, but the multiple deities in Skyrim actually help me remember how little sense it makes for there to be multiple "truths" that are true. If a Nord warrior who worships Stendarr gets taken out by a member of the Bark brotherhood after promising themselves to a Daedric Prince, where do they go?? This kind of confusion would be everyday reality if there were multiple religions that were equally true. It also would make no sense for each way to be an "equal way to God" because it would mean things that definitely get us away from God in one religion is what gets us closer to God in others. And it would be even more confusing for people who change religions. But the truth is that there is one way, and we can try to come up with equally true deities, but they can't coexist as truths.

So while people CAN believe whatever they want, just like the people of Skyrim worship different pantheons and even individuals within a pantheon, but it's up to us to speak the truth in love (Ephesians 4:15), talk to them as ambassadors for Christ (2 Corinthians 5:18–21), begging them to get on the life raft instead of drowning rather than, as some seem to do, yelling and demanding to join our side or we'll blast them because that's not going to convince them we're sharing truth. We can make this bold statement because while every other religion says "Here's god / gods / no god, earn your way to heaven / hell / nirvana / moksha / not being labeled a bad person with outweighing your bad with good if you haven't done certain bad things," but Jesus says, "You could never pay for the wrong you've done, so I paid for you before you asked and when you didn't deserve it, and you just have to believe that I'm the one who did it, that I did it, and that I mean it when I say I'm the only way" (John 14:6, Romans 5:8).

Then there are just plain Bible verses in some games like Fallout 3, and while the game uses it as a reason for pursuing clean water, it literally told millions of people the gospel by quoting Revelation 21:6 "I am the Alpha and the Omega, the beginning and the end. To the thirsty, I will give from the spring of the water of life without payment." And they may just hear it and play on, but it gives us a chance to share that gospel while we play and remind us that we need to be focused on Scripture because even game characters recognize following the Bible can change the world for the better. It also may show us how that's a verse we may not have read otherwise, so there's a lot in the Bible that we can miss if we aren't reading the whole thing consistently.

In Dishonored, the choices we make change the game's endings and can make the entire city a darker place or solve a lot of the problems in the city. Real life is like that, we have more choices than we admit in making our world darker or lighter. But we usually see our life as a routine and leave the "big" events to the video games or world leaders. I've said it before, we are not some random NPC to God. He has plans for us to make the world a better place, but our enemy is relying on us to keep our head down and let the world get darker, ignoring those in need and those who need help, keeping silent instead of listening and speaking, hitting a like button instead of doing something to change a situation. We may not be an elite super soldier or an expert assassin or the Hero of Time, but we can still do things daily to make a real difference if we are open to it and look for it.

In Knights of the Old Republic and other games with a light/dark good/evil meter I play good, asking to the best of the game code's ability "What Would Jesus Do?" but I also playthrough the dark/evil choices for achievements but consciously think of the Bible and how the opposite is what I should do if that was a real situation. While most of us make excuses when we make choices, we know would put our alignment toward the dark/evil side, games like this can be a wake-up call to see just how important those little choices are to who we are and who the world around us sees us as. It feels like small acts to us, but the same things we make excuses for can either pull us down darker paths or cause other believers to stumble by our actions. In a sad irony, some people who claim to be Christians but were hurt by Christians being two-faced do a lot of things themselves that make others hurt. We need to make the choice to be different and evaluate our choices, using the Bible to see if our decisions would draw us closer to God or push us further away.

Some games can be therapeutic and give us time that can include thinking about the Bible. Some examples of this for me are Animal Crossing and Harvest Moon. The simplicity of the games is engaging enough to be a lot of fun, and there's always things to do, but the games don't require as much concentration as other games and give my mind freedom to wander. Wandering minds have been the excuse of a lot of us for wrong thoughts and actions, but when we give our brain a direction to wander in, it can help us think about Jesus more. Even some open world games that require concentration at times, but also have a lot of time to wander, can be like this some of the time, like Breath of the Wild, Skyrim, Oblivion, FFX, etc. There's been good portions of this book that have been mulled over while playing these very games!

Online games can be Easter eggs in that they give us platforms to witness to people we'd never meet otherwise. I've met people from all over the world playing games, and I've been able to have some really good conversations just linking things in the games to the gospel in one way or another. Much like parts of this book have been, God's truth connects to every need we have, and every desire of our hearts, and every fear we have. Sharing the Bible verses online can also help us memorize them as we type them out over and over.

Of course, there's also some Christian-based video games on the Bible, Bible stories, or Christian books. These would obviously help us learn Bible stories and Bible principles if they are accurate, but many have a reputation for being cheesy or bad quality, and others are just "Bible themed" but not biblical at all. Sometimes, the cheesy but accurate game can be just what we need though if we still want to play games but are working through some of the previously mentioned sins that, personally, would require a break from certain games.

We can also do this for real world things as well! God made the entire world and is the author and perfecter of our faith (Hebrews

12:2), so all he made has echoes of him even when we take into account the brokenness sin brought into the equation. And just like I mentioned before with creation telling us who God is, simple things like a walk can be great times with God and have great Easter eggs to share him with ourselves and with others if we take the time to look for him and think about him.

It's not as hard as we make it to see God's Easter eggs. They are all around through the real world and the digital worlds. We just have to take the time and thought to make those connections real in our minds and in our hearts rather than think our spiritual lives are separate from the rest of our lives for some reason. Our entire lives should be "in the world but not of it" (John 17:14–19), not just our life at church. So, that means even in our video game playing, we should be glorifying God by finding and sharing these Easter eggs and putting them at the forefront of our games rather than thinking we have to stop our games to "be spiritual."

These are just a *few* examples, so I hope between the little connections of games in this chapter and throughout this book as a whole are proof enough that we can do it. And if anyone we encounter still thinks that following Jesus and playing video games are incompatible, I hope this chapter will help them see otherwise.

Chapter Questions

1. What's your favorite video game Easter egg?
2. What was the most surprising Easter egg in this chapter?
3. What is one way you can make the world a little better?
4. What are some habits you need to change so you can do everything for God's glory?
5. Have you ever done evangelism online?

Achievement Unlocked:
RABBITS AND CHICKENS

CHAPTER 10

Unlocking Achievements

There's just something about that little noise, followed by a notification popping up, that just makes us happy. There're different names for it, achievements, trophies, challenges, medals, badges, stamps, and more, going all the way back to simple "high scores," but they all give that same feeling. A few major systems/games don't have them, so it's understandable to not know that feeling, but some of us choose a system solely based on the achievement system, and some of my systems that don't use achievements I only have because I really wanted a game that was only for that system. These achievements do a lot. They encourage multiple playthroughs by needing to do the same quest in different ways. They encourage multiple playthroughs because we missed them on one go-through. They encourage us to branch out by playing a mode we wouldn't normally play (single player in largely multiplayer games or vice versa). They keep the game going long after we finished the main story of the game.

While I've argued in my own life that things would be a lot more interesting if we had real-world achievements that would pop up after certain events, that hasn't happened yet (but with real-life HUD style glasses getting developed, who knows). But that's where a little creativity comes in! Our achievements are our purpose, our gifts, creating our own achievements, and using what we have for Jesus.

Our purpose is an achievement because it's something we have to unlock, we usually don't just wake up and find out we're supposed to save the world from some alien invasion or anything like that. Unlike in video games, we have to find out what we're supposed to do with our lives. And while some of us have only gotten the joke achievements for messing things up too many times so far in life, that's where God comes in with help, grace, and making things different! Sometimes, it's a little easy because we can just direct the things we like to do into a job or hobby that meets our purpose. Other times, finding our purpose can be difficult because sometimes we don't know ourselves well enough to know what we should be doing in life or we have so many things we enjoy that we're not sure what direction to go. Our purpose is part of who we really are, kind of like how technically a lamp in a video game uses real-world electricity to run. It doesn't always show itself instantly, but by getting to know God and ourselves better, we can find it.

So, how do we find our purpose?

Everyone has two parts to their purpose, and ours is no different.

The first part is a universal purpose that applies to everyone regardless of who they are, where they are from, and when they were born. That purpose is to know God and to make him known. We may know God in the salvation sense, we are all supposed to *be knowing* him better and better as well. We are also supposed to make him known to others, getting people a little closer to Jesus, no matter how close or how far they are in the first place.

The second part of that purpose is much more specific, how God wants us to use what we have to make him known and what we are supposed to be doing specifically. This part can change in looks as we age and by what jobs and hobbies we have. And while this looks different for everyone, there are some things about it that are also universal, in that it is part of who we are even when circumstances change.

For example, from my life, my purpose is to teach, and that's always looked different in my life. I have always been an introvert, but God has always still used me for that purpose. Even before Jesus, I liked to help people learn history. Then when I got saved, I have loved to help people learn things about God and help them find out more about God. In college, I was a prayer leader who taught the

Bible weekly, then I was a spiritual life director that taught prayer leaders about the Bible and about how to reach the Bible. Then I was a missionary to Thailand, and I taught people English because that's something that really helped improve their quality of life, and I got to teach them about Jesus at the same time because I could bridge the gospel to teaching English. Then when God called me back to America, I became a history teacher, and because all of history shows Jesus, and how when we follow him in word only or not at all, it makes all sorts of problems, it was easy to bridge it to knowing God as well. And obviously by this book, I'm still teaching about Jesus, even in the context of video games.

Your purpose might not be the same as mine, but it is a good example of how our purpose will stay the same even if the expression of that purpose changes. There's any number of purposes, so I can't give a specific universal way to FIND that beyond the guideline I've said, but the next achievement can help.

Our gifts that God gave us is an achievement because they are one of the ways we can find our purposes, but they are also just ways that we can serve God and serve people. Only one of my gifts is teaching, but I've learned it's my purpose through time and knowing Jesus more that there are plenty of other gifts I have, and I'm sure all of us are the same. We have a variety of gifts, but all of them come from God. We can develop some of them, and even use some of them for less than godly means, but he is the source of them all.

There are some gifts that are not spiritual in nature, but because we have one life, the division between "spiritual" and "physical" are, again, artificial. For example, there're many gifted athletes that are the furthest thing from godly, but God still gave them their gifts, and they are going to have to answer for how they used those gifts. Compare this to other athletes who know God and know their purpose, and they use that gift of athletic ability to spread the gospel and support God's work.

Other gifts are even called "spiritual gifts," and they are more obviously from God because they seem spiritual in nature. These are listed in three main passages as well as five other verses with gifts listed. Of course, these are not "all inclusive" but are broad enough we can be confident we have some of these gifts.

I'm going to start with 1 Corinthians 12 because it uses these gifts to illustrate who we all are, one body in Christ. None of us have all the gifts, and none of us get to decide which ones we have (even if we can pray for some) because the Holy Spirit is the one who decides it for us. The gifts Paul mentions here are administration, apostle, discernment, faith, healings, helps, knowledge, miracles, prophecy, teaching, tongues, interpretation of tongues, and wisdom.

Administration is the ability to run things smoothly, see how to maximize potential, spot and work out problems, and run things well. It doesn't always mean we are the boss, but it can mean that or can include things like an administrative assistant or secretaries.

Apostle is not the same as the twelve Apostles because that criteria is listed in Acts 1 of seeing Jesus while he was alive and him risen, but I use the distinction of them being the "capital A, Apostles" while this is the "lowercased a, apostles." This comes from the Greek meaning "sent one" and can refer to those called to be missionaries, which we have domestic missionaries called to other areas of a country with the gospel, or international missionaries called to other countries with the gospel. I've been both of those, and it's definitely a gift!

Discernment is the ability to know when something is true or not and goes from people's hearts to spirits to other such things, and while it can be our gift, we also have to always be careful to balance between trusting our gift and not using it to write someone off without giving them a fair chance because they rub us the wrong way.

Faith is a gift because it comes easy to some people to trust God for big things and in big ways, but this is one gift that we all have as believers, but how easy it is to exercise is where it's a gift, much like how every human without a disability can run, but we can't be professional runners without a gift for it and training.

Healing is one of the controversial gifts because of the multiple people who use it not only in an unbiblical way but claim some special spiritual authority over others because of it and use it as an excuse for their unbiblical lifestyles. Real healing is easy to see because it is (a) from God, (b) scientifically verifiable that the person had the ailment before the healing, (c) scientifically verifiable that they no longer have the ailment after the healing, and (d) used for God's glory rather than to convince people to give money to the one using the gift. If someone has the genuine gift of healing, they don't act like it comes from them and don't act like it gives them a license to be the boss of a place for their gift. Paul is a good example of this because even when the church in Corinth wasn't financially supporting him, he healed and then didn't bring it up as a reason for them to support him nor did he hold meetings for it or heal everyone every time (2 Timothy 4:20).

Helps is being gifted at helping people, which sounds simple, but is a gift because we not only have the desire and ability to help but in the right ways at the right time for the situation to help people know Jesus better even behind the scenes. For example, I knew some people who thought this was their gift because they always washed dishes at a church function and no one argued about it because dishes were being washed, but when I worked with them one time, it was clear helps was not their gifting but that they just didn't want to do anything where people could see them and didn't want to talk to anyone but the other dishwasher, so they were being selfish and antisocial but could pass it off as a gift because no one else was volunteering.

Knowledge is not being smarter than anyone else but having a natural gift to learn things well and more importantly be able to share it at the right time to help others grow in their knowledge.

Miracles is another controversial one but again should be easy and clear that any miracle claimed to be done is done for God rather than the reputation of the one doing it, making the lost who see it more convinced of God rather than more skeptical and not done for money or behind closed doors.

Prophecy has gotten a lot of confusion over the years as people got prophets and fortune tellers mixed up. Even Old Testament prophets were not people who could "see the future" but rather people who were listening to God and telling what he said. They were more like preachers than future tellers, and more importantly, what they said when it did involve the future ALWAYS came true.

Deuteronomy 13 even gives a criterion for testing a prophet, by checking if what they say comes true, not in a vague way but specifically true, and then says not only to not listen to any prophet who is not one hundred percent accurate but in the Mosaic Law they were supposed to be stoned. So, if anyone claims to be a prophet as their gift but is every wrong even slightly, we are supposed to call them out as fake and never listen to them again even if we "like" them and have followed them for a long time thinking they were right. Paul says that this is important because what makes a prophet is that they hear from GOD and say what HE says, not whatever THEY want to say, and even God's Word needs to be said in God's time. Hananiah, the false prophet, found this out when he spoke that God would break Babylon's yoke and return the exiles but was giving false prophecies about how, when, and with who, and Jeremiah had to say what God was REALLY saying, and it ended BADLY for Hananiah (Jeremiah 28).

Teaching is the gift to make complex ideas simple and communicate that in a way that others can understand and know the material. We've all had teachers that couldn't actually do that, and it makes school miserable, and we've all had people who knew a lot but couldn't communicate it well, so we never understood them, that's why it's a gift.

Tongues is the last of the controversial ones, and it's the ability to speak different languages, and from the context of Acts, it's ones that were never studied before and as a sign to show being filled with the Holy Spirit. But the key is that they are spoken so those in that language can know what God is saying without an interpreter, and in a church setting in 1 Corinthians 14, Paul says that only two or three should ever do it in a service, and only if there is someone to interpret it, or they should be quiet because it doesn't build anyone up if they don't know what's going on.

Interpretation of tongues comes into play as how it should work in 1 Corinthians 14 as well, where they are needed for someone to speak in tongues in a church service or the one with the gift of tongues shouldn't do it. It's the natural ability to know what's going on in a language that's not been studied; sometimes they seem like they're just "good at context," but they usually know, even if for just one language, what people are saying without needing it translated. They may not be able to say anything back, but they know what's being said.

Wisdom is putting knowledge into practice. Both for ourselves and for others; those with this gift can see how to implement things and when and where to say things so that it's received the best. They're the people we want to help us when we know the right thing to do but aren't sure how to do it.

Romans 12:3–8 is the second passage about gifts, listing exhortation, giving, leadership, mercy, prophecy, service, and teaching as gifts.

Exhortation is the ability to communicate ideas that draw people to action, like a lot of preachers who seem to be gifted at getting people to follow their sermons rather than just listen to them. It's getting people to not only hear us but follow what ideas we have.

Giving is another gift we are all supposed to do to an extent, but as a gift, it means having an ability to find places that need the gift, giving when it's needed, and giving what is needed, all with a passion to give.

Leadership is a little bit of exhortation and a little bit of administration. Getting people to follow us while being able to organize them into good ways to work.

Mercy is having a heart for those who mess up and being able to both empathize with their thick skulls while helping them see the need to get out of their bad habits even while being patient with their long roads to recovery.

Prophecy, we talked about before, so I won't repeat, and service is another name for "helps," and teaching, I also went over.

Ephesians 4:11–12 is the last passage that lists gifts, and it gives apostles, evangelists, prophets, shepherds, and teachers as different types of people to equip each other and general believers for ministry, so instead, I'll get to some gifts listed in various passages. These are celibacy, hospitality, marriage, martyrdom, speaking, and voluntarily being in poverty.

Celibacy seems to be one of the most dreaded and least appreciated gifts in modern times. It's still a gift some of us have, and according to Paul, it's even one we should want (Matthew 19:12, 1 Corinthians 7). Although I personally am glad to be talking about it from the married side, it's not something that's a curse or against us. Some of us have it for only a season, preparing us for the person we should be in marriage. For some, it's a lifetime gift that, in the world, means they are lonely and awkward, but according to Scripture, it's meant as a gift to help us work better for the kingdom and be able to go anywhere for God at the drop of a hat. Of course, the world likes to take God's gifts and make them look less than desirable, but God is good and he doesn't give junk.

Hospitality is a gift that some see as exclusively for extroverts. However, it's more of a heart to find those who don't feel at home at a church or in their home and make them feel more comfortable, so anyone who is thoughtful can have this gift. Hebrews 13:2 says, "Do not neglect to show hospitality to strangers, for thereby some have entertained angels unawares." So, this is another gift that we all are supposed to practice, even if we don't have the *gift* of it."

Marriage is also a spiritual gift and while many people get into it without thinking of it as a gift or thinking about it beyond being someone they feel strongly for. But marriage is not meant for everyone as the divorce rate shows. Jesus said it himself in Matthew 19:10–12 way before our modern society because marriage is meant to be for life, choosing love and forgiveness over selfishness, sin, and bitterness. And while not all people are called to marriage, it's also not an excuse to be with people outside marriage (Galatians 5:19–21, Colossians 3:5–6).

1 Peter 4:10–11 calls speaking a spiritual gift, and it doesn't mean just communicating but the gift of communication similar to teaching and preaching and prophecy but different in that it's conveying meaning rather than information and messages.

Suffering is one surprising spiritual gift because many acts like suffering disproves God himself. Our sinful world that we messed up (and still choose sin and mess up more) means that suffering will exist, but it means something different as a spiritual gift. Acts 5:41,

James 1:2, and 1 Peter 3:13–17 all shows that when we suffer *for Jesus*, then it is a gift. While we generally don't enjoy suffering, it takes a special gift of the Holy Spirit to know someone can endure it. It is a gift because it's not the norm for us, and the most we usually experience is light mockery, if that. But the early church felt this gift in mass, and it made the church as a whole better for it, and the response of faith in the midst of suffering for the faith made the early church explode with believers because it was hard to argue with their hearts enduring it with joy. And in the persecuted church today, it remains a huge way people come to Christ.

Martyrdom is the only gift most people would choose celibacy over even compared to suffering. Because it doesn't sound like most people's goal is life, but it is for some. Matthew 5:11 and 1 Peter 4:12–19 show that we will face persecutions when we are standing up for truth, but there's an even more special gift of being one called to give their life for the gospel. Revelation 12:11 even says that these believers have a special part in Christ conquering Satan. Psalm 116:15 shows us that when we die for him, it's precious to him. *Foxe's Book of Martyrs* shows that this has been not only a common gift through church history, but in the early church, it was very frequent, and in modern times, there are organizations like the Voice of the Martyrs that show it's still a gift for today.

We often choose to make a big sacrifice in games because "it's just a game," and even if it gets particularly emotional to do, we choose to make that sacrifice "to save the world." In Christ, it can be a very similar situation, and we need to be ready in faith in case it ever gets to that point because it's a gift we never know we have until we need it and use it and then we're front and center in the line of Jesus's victory tour. 1 Peter 4:12–19 and 1 Corinthians 13:3 do show us one important reminder though: it doesn't count for God if we're sinning so we're suffering or if we are trying to get glory and fame by giving our lives for Jesus. As strange as it sounds, apparently, some people were either trying to do it or were actually doing it if Peter and Paul both needed to warn about it. It all comes down to actually believing Philippians 1:21 is true when it says, "For to me to live is Christ and to die is gain."

The last gift we'll look at is voluntarily being in poverty. It's mentioned in Acts 4:32–37 and 1 Corinthians 13:3, and it's a heart that knows God wants them to give away earthly possessions to an extreme, not to look "more holy" or to "be holier" but to be using one's giftings and have temptations of materialism gone. It's not to be taken lightly because it is voluntary, and God isn't calling people who will use it as an excuse to complain. Jesus even tried to call a rich man to this gift, but he cared about his stuff more, and it was a sad story in the gospels (Matthew 19:16–30). This also doesn't mean we are poor because we've spent all our money on the latest system and on every game we can get our hands on.

So, which gifts do we have?

Some gifts are as obvious to us as crouching means we're in stealth mode while others take some time and thought to notice that we have them. Since God is the one who gave us those gifts though, he's interested in helping us find them. And while using our gifts should be as easy as facing a hoard of enemies with the best weapons and armor while with the easiest settings, it doesn't mean that those gifts feel easy all the time. To use myself as an example again, while my gift is teaching, because of the whole introverted thing, I have to be careful not to run myself ragged teaching at every opportunity because I need to take time alone to recharge and refocus. To find out what gifts we have, there are multiple spiritual gift tests we can take, and I've included some links to some of them currently running in chapter 13. Others we'll find as we go through life, like certain achievements that we only unlock by doing something random we never would have thought of as achievement worthy.

The Holy Spirit won't yell "Hey! Listen!" and bounce around as a ball of light at an important target or over which gift is ours, but we can learn to listen to him and hear his voice inside us that reminds us of truth (John 14:26), encourages us (Acts 9:31, Romans 8:26–27), warns us (Nehemiah 9:30), or convicts us (John 16:8). We need to listen to him and not ignore him because that will only dull our hearing him the next time until we can barely hear him without some serious repentance (Ephesians 4:30, 2 Timothy 4:3–4).

Another thing we can do is make achievements for ourselves, like the end of each chapter here. We can come up with things we know we should be accomplishing and make them for that. I enjoy doing this and even make the little noises when I know I've just accomplished something on my personal achievement list. Some we can try examples, many of which I have done in the past, including finishing the whole Bible, beating a temptation, getting a job we enjoy, finding a good church, getting married (if called to that), getting baptized (if we haven't yet and are a believer), getting a certain number of items in a collection of ours, betting a certain number of video games, reading a certain number of books, publishing a book about Jesus AND video games (wink wink), to name a few, and I'll add some more for us to try out in the last chapter.

Another achievement is using our platforms for ministry. We all have something we're good at and something we have to do consistently. God gave us those things to use as a platform for telling others about him. It could be a business, a job, social media, video games, our life situation, or even a call to a specific ministry like preaching or evangelism or missions. Whatever we find is our consistent way to interact with others, that's how we should be reaching out to tell them about Jesus.

We don't have to be as loud as a new hand touching the beacon or the batteries in our remote being low, and we don't have to be obnoxious about it either. The less obnoxious and the more earnest we are, the better it works usually. It should be a natural part of our conversations. It's not for most of us, but that's because we've kept Jesus separate from the other things we enjoy for so long that it's strange for them to mix.

It's kind of like having two game consoles, but if we get a few new games for one and not the other, it starts to feel odd when we pick up the other controller (or keyboard). But the more we use both and the less we see them as one OR the other, the easier it is to seamlessly switch between the two (except, of course, during quick time events when our brains instantly forget every single button combination of every single controller we've ever held).

All these things, our unique purpose, our spiritual gifts, our own personally created achievements, and our distinct platforms, work together for us to discover and then unlock our achievements in Christ.

Chapter Questions

1. Do you know your purpose?
If not, what things from this chapter have helped you narrow it down?
2. What are some of your gifts?
3. Have you ever taken a spiritual gifts test?
If not, see chapter 13 for some suggested ones.
4. Have you ever unlocked any of the achievements I listed?
5. What are some achievements you want to unlock?

Achievement Unlocked:
REDUNDANCY IS OKAY

CHAPTER 11

Cheat Codes and Mods

Some of us genuinely enjoy finding and using cheat codes and mods. And while we shouldn't use them in multiplayer (so we don't get banned or put into a server with only other modders and cheaters like in Titanfall), in some games, they can make the whole experience more fun when we feel like we've mastered the game or have gotten tired of certain bugs. We've talked about the negative use of them by n00bs, but this is the fun kind of cheats and mods in single player to make the game more immersive and fun when we acknowledge the use of mods and talk about how fun and funny some of them are. We're going to be looking at some of these in our spiritual lives where we can add some things to help us learn things faster, easier, or in a more fun way to help us get these practices down and grow faster.

Sometimes, using too many or the wrong kind of hacks, cheat codes, and mods can make the game more confusing than a Mass Effect ending. And it's like that for us in our lives as well. There are things we can do to help our spiritual growth and life, but too many of them at once can just get us confused and overwhelmed (like an old PC with so many mods the FPS is more like frames per hour). So, while these are all good things to add to life, it's important to pace ourselves and take our time settling into them and seeing what makes things more enjoyable and which things would be too much to add to our lives.

One of my first and favorite mods is listening to our Bible as we play. There are some great audio Bibles online, many of which have some interesting voices and make it interesting to listen to. Doing this really helps us get the Bible into our minds and hearts even while we're playing, and there are even times where we hear something that makes us have to pause to look up the reference and read it more ourselves. I've been able to listen to some books, like Philippians, several times in one night while I was playing, and it really helps with memorization and hearing the big picture. There are some games where we feel like we need to listen to the game itself, but from experience, there isn't a lot we need to hear to be able to play a game we've played more than once, and even games that are stealthier don't need the sound as often as we think. We can even do things like adding a reminder alarm on our phone to read or listen to the Bible, to take away the excuses we sometimes use.

Another good mod is listening to Christian music as we play. There are a lot of great songs based on the Bible, and the truths in those songs can act as extra help in growing our faith if we listen and apply them. Some of my earliest discipleship was listening to music like Steven Curtis Chapman and David Crowder and Josh Wilson, and they taught me a lot of how to be a Christian before I knew what I was doing and how to walk the walk. Some of us are in churches that don't match our musical styles, but there is good and true Christian music that spans every genre and style so we can listen and praise and worship in whatever style suits us best. This music can really expand what we know about the Bible, Jesus, and what we should do in response to the gospel. There is even a Christian artist called KJ-52 with a song called "Video Games" that makes a lot of funny comparisons to Jesus and video games.

Similar to that, we can hack our game's code by taking the phrases or events that are super repetitive and use them to our advantage. Every game with any kind of dialogue or music has it, and we all have some that are comical, painful, or hilarious to hear burned into our memories. It may be just how many guards had their careers altered by an oddly specific arrow injury, being told to "get over here," being asked "would you kindly…," hearing "Game Set," the princess is in another castle, having to gather your party before you can keep going, gaining and losing a command center, loading screens, being asked to fetch a random item, the batteries in our remote being low, or if the games we are playing are really hard (or if we just stink): game over. All these give us an audio cue that we can use to remind us to pray. Think of how often we hear those phrases or sounds and, therefore, how many times we'd be praying a day if we prayed every time we heard those! Talk about leveling up our prayer life!

Another mod is finding people to regularly share with. We have a lot we can share, and a lot we need to share: our testimony, what we're learning, our struggles so others can help us through them, the gospel to those who aren't believers. Where and how we share doesn't matter as much as that we share, in person or online. We also don't have to worry that we're not "professionals" when sharing with others because Paul says in 2 Timothy 4:5, "Do the work of an evangelist," not the BE an evangelist. It all comes down to being willing to share whatever God has done for us. Much of the time it's just being confident enough in God to share what he's done and not worry as much as giving a three-point sermon or writing enough to fill the code book of a PS4 game.

Also, there are mods to memorize Bible verses to help when we're in a situation to remember them rather than have to go look them up. Sometimes, it's to share it with others but more often it's to remind ourselves of truth so we don't go sprinting into sin like it's a pre-order game we've waited three years for. These are not all the ways to memorize, but these are some that have worked well for me in the past. And don't forget the method mentioned in chapter 4 to practice a verse after dying in a game.

Saying the verse out loud over and over is the simplest, and can be done most anywhere we don't feel too odd about talking out loud, and can be done even while playing a game. It also helps to read the verse in different or funny accents or in the voice of our favorite game characters (who actually talk, saying it as Link probably won't help us remember John 3:16 if we're just saying "Hyut, hyut, hyaaah!"). Writing it on a whiteboard-type surface and then erasing words, repeating the entire phrase each time we erase is also good for more visual learners. One of the best ways to get a verse into my head is teaching them to others because when I'm teaching it, I feel the importance of remembering it, and it helps it stick in my memory. Some of us learn better with music, so we can make up a song to go with each verse or a group of verses. Hand motions or moving can also be helpful for those who like to learn physically. Sometime, it's helpful to connect Bible verses to video games, such as Fallout 3 helping me memorize Revelation 21:6, even sometimes though if game is doing opposite of the point of the verse, such as quoting Romans 12:19 "Beloved, never avenge yourselves but leave it to the wrath of God, for it is written, 'Vengeance is mine, I will repay, says the Lord'" while playing Fable 2 or God of War.

Some mods make the game more fun than naming our Pokémon rival "idiot," and there are going to be some fun mods for ourselves as well. Our lives don't have to be boring to follow Jesus well, and no one who has a healthy relationship with God would say that their spiritual life is boring. So, we're going to look at ways to enjoy our life with Christ as well.

The biggest mod of this type is just to think of how to have fun with God. Christianity is a relationship, and while he is God and we need to respect him, he's also supposed to be our closest friend and first love (James 2:23, Revelation 2:4–5). So, we need to think about things we would normally do with friends. Dance, even, and for some of us especially, if we're alone with God because it's just fun and funny but also a way to worship (Psalm 87:7, Psalm 149:3, Psalm 150:4). We can also not just sing to worship God but sing with him because he is singing over us (Zephaniah 3:17). Take time to laugh with God because most of us remember times with friends that make us laugh, tell jokes, funny stories, reminisce a little of comical situation because he's been with us through all of them (Genesis 17:17, Genesis 21:6, Job 8:21, Psalm 126:2, Ecclesiastes 3:4, Luke 6:21). We can also tell him about what game we're playing and why we like it, like a real friend who we actually believe exists, and our video game commentary would probably benefit from that reminder. If it feels odd to be talking to God like that, just think of it as talking to a friend on a headset while playing, and even wear one if it helps it feel more natural.

We can also mod our lives by having fun with God by running around and having fun outside. I personally would never suggest running as an activity to have fun, but to each their own. Some of us need to get outside a little more anyway, but the point is to do things where we get into locations that remind us of who he is and that he's with us. We can take a hike in the woods, walk along the beach, walk around our neighborhoods, climb trees or rock walls, let go of (biodegradable) balloons with a letter to God, and be our own character running through the wilds (just don't bring an actual battle axe to the park, that's generally frowned upon unless it's foam and we're LARPing).

We mostly just need to be creative, like the premise of any good mod, and look for what seems to be "lacking" in the base "game" to fix it. Some of the most creative people in the world are game designers and game players. We just need to have the mindset of RPwG (role-playing with God) and ask what we would do if we acted like God was physically with us…the way he actually is. For example, any game that's remotely popular has an abundance of fan art. It's not by professionals or the game designers, but it's by the regular gamers who just enjoy the game itself and the characters. Just like that, us regular Christians don't need to be deep theologians with multiple PhDs to do stuff for God and to have thoughts about him. Sometimes, it's like when we have a younger sibling and we just unplugged the controller so they feel like they're playing; we just have to be trying, and God takes care of the rest.

Another mod is to visit multiple biblical churches every few months or so. While we should definitely be faithful if we have a good biblical church, but sometimes, finding another nice church that believes in and lives the Bible but has a different service order and different style of worship is good to mix things up and keep us engaged. I've even found that sometimes when I accidentally find a bad church visiting others, it makes me more thankful for the one I attend. And when I've found other good churches, I still fully support my church while having more ministries I can pray for and support as I'm able.

Some mods in games add things we definitely don't need, and shouldn't want, and can make it feel like the game waits from someone else to walk in then has worse timing than when it's 3:00 a.m. and we turn off our DS and Mario yells "Bye-bye!" loud enough to wake everyone in the neighborhood up. So, it's important to get those out of the way and out of our game.

One we should avoid is choosing to sin, and instead of trying to quit the sin, we try to justify it by saying things like "everybody sins" or "it's not like I am (fill in sin that is 'worse' than the one we're doing)" to distract from the fact we're just not trying to get rid of it very hard (if at all). Of course, we've all either done it, or lied about not doing it, but we need to recognize that sin is sin, and just because we're not trained assassins doesn't mean we can overlook our sins.

Along the same lines, we shouldn't say we are "struggling" with a sin that we're not doing anything to stop. It's only actually "struggling" with a sin if we are actually trying to resist it. We need to actively be resisting it as Job 11:14 says, "If iniquity is in your hand, put it far away and let not injustice dwell in your tents." We avoid dealing with the roots of our sin because "Jesus forgave them already." Proverbs 28:13 says, "Whoever conceals his transgressions will not prosper, but he who confesses and forsakes them will obtain mercy." So, we don't conceal our sins but instead we confess our sin to Jesus and work through our sins. We should also avoid trying to sound more spiritual than we are, and if we've never done it, we've seen plenty of examples for sure. We need to think of ourselves as we really are; God isn't impressed with how we pretend to be, he cares about our heart, and any benefit of pretending to be spiritual ends as soon as someone else is "noticing" (Matthew 6:1–2, 1 Corinthians 11:31–32, Galatians 6:5).

Another mod to avoid is knowing the right things to do and ignoring them because it's just like doing the wrong things in the first place (James 4:17). It's the same as wishing good for someone when we're perfectly capable of helping them and then doing nothing to make a difference about it; it shows our faith is not only small, it's dead (James 2:14–17). It's also like trying to earn salvation, it just doesn't help because it can't be done (Ephesians 2:8–9, 1 John 2:1–2).

Some people also like to make their own mods, but some things we shouldn't make as mods include making our walk with Jesus mental activity instead of a full-body activity (Luke 10:27). Yes, we need to mentally believe in Jesus, but we can't just leave it at a mental exercise because that's not faith. Like believing a chair can be sat in doesn't help us have a seat until we actually put our body into it. We also shouldn't make personal preferences become issues we think affect other people's salvation (Romans 14). We all have things we prefer over others: types of consoles, fantasy vs. sci-fi, RPG vs. FPS, online vs. alone, kosher vs. all food vs. vegetarian vs. non-GMO, fancy clothes vs. casual for church. We may feel like these are strong issues for us personally, but people can be Christians and be a lot of different things from each other. That's why God made a lot of different local churches, but we are all part of the Church, his body. Convictions are worth standing for and defending why we do them, but they are personal and don't affect salvation. Preferences are okay to have, but they are just what we like.

Similar to that, we shouldn't make debating over pointless things a habit. Some things are important to argue about, some are actually fun to argue about and the other person is having fun as well, but some things are absolutely unproductive. Yelling at people and debating angrily almost never actually changes people's views on the subject, especially if it's about a personal preference. So, we need to speak the truth in love, as stated before, but we also need to be mindful about how and when we get into discussions about things and if they are productive discussions instead of actual fights.

These mods take away a lot from us, but thankfully, they are not a permanent download. Much like our sins, we can (with some time, energy, and a little patience with ourselves) get these mods out of our game. We can also take the time to get the good ones into our files, and our lives will be a little easier, a little nicer, and more like Jesus in the end. Don't forget to think of personal mods that will benefit as well because no matter how many mods exist, even how many good mods exist, there is always another that we can add to our mods.

That's how we use mods and cheat codes in our real life, and next, we get to head into an open world of our own.

Chapter Questions

1. Have you ever listened to the Bible as you played video games before?
2. Which mod do you want to "install" the most?
3. What is a "fun" mod you enjoy?
4. What mods do you need to uninstall?
5. How do you feel about mods in video games?

Achievement Unlocked:
BUTTON MASHING WORKS

CHAPTER 12
Your MMORPG

Some of us don't realize it, but we are part of our own MMORPG, and each part of that acronym can help us know a little more about who we are and how to interact in that aspect of our personal lives beyond the games.

MASSIVE

Some of us have a hard time interacting with others for a variety of reasons, but we can't just hide in a cardboard box or a barrel from God or from the lost world that needs to hear about him. We have to step out into the world and choose those interactions. Starting with the interactions we already take part in regularly. It may be a few people we already see or talk to daily. It may be people mostly online at first. But we need to reach out and show who Jesus is to them with our words and our actions. Even if that means saying sorry for some of the less-than-Jesus decisions we've made and actions we've done. We can also be mindful of our daily interactions to show God's love in the little things we do and say and to be kind to those around us.

The world is full of reminders of God for us to keep him in our mind as well as point others to him. Creation itself points to him, and the beauty, complexity, and goodness in the world are easy reminders of how good God is and what he has for us. But, unfortunately, the world is also full of reminders of just how far it has fallen.

Even without dark video games, the world has plenty of darkness that reminds us of the fall and how it impacts our everyday lives. From sins people do to each other from their choices to sicknesses and natural disasters that leave death and pain and suffering in their wake, we can see just how bad things are. While some people see this a TKO for God being real, it actually makes the most sense from the Bible's perspective. God made our world without any of that, but since he gave us free will, he chose not to let himself force us to only do good. That free will of ours started to sin from Adam and Eve, and ever since then, we certainly choose to sin daily on our own. That made the world itself messed up with things like sickness and natural disasters, in addition to the human element of suffering. So, as long as we have free will, we do our own parts to make the world the way it is with suffering.

As Christians who saw the opening cut scene of humanity and why things are so messed up, we expect to see it and are supposed to be a small part of the solution by choosing God's way and not contributing to the sin problem as much as we can and working to help get others out of sin. Sickness and death will still be around until Jesus returns, but we can do our part to make it better. It's massive, but with God, we can do it. And while our lives in video games may be underrated by many who don't get it, our lives in the real world are sometimes underrated by ourselves because we don't see just how massive things are and how massive of a difference we can make while still enjoying our games to the full. Because this world is massive!

MULTIPLAYER

We have a lot of open-world interactions, and often, we go through those interactions with the excitement of a game we've played for ten years. But that's where we miss God. There may be a lot of little details in our day, but our little details are reminders of a big God behind them. While some of us have a hard time getting through books like Leviticus and Numbers, those books are really important in showing the tiny details God pays attention to. It may seem hard to read about what kind of clothes ancient Israeli priests were supposed to wear under their priestly robes (Leviticus 6:10 if that peaked anyone's curiosity), but it shows just how much God pays attention to the little details and cares. That's important for us because that means the things we feel like no one else cares about because it's too small of a detail is something God cares infinitely about because he cares for us! Every little interaction, every stress, every boredom, every fear, we can give it all to him because of his care for us (1 Peter 5:7).

Because he cares, that means we have a lot of choices we wouldn't have. We can think through our dialogue options before we say them, and we can choose kindness when we want to respond with hate toward others or ourselves. We can choose goodness over cutting others or ourselves down. We can choose responding in love rather than responding in selfishness. These aren't always easy choices, but they are the better choices. If anyone needs help seeing they are the better choices, we just have to look at video games again; the characters we love playing are the ones who give themselves to beating the selfish and shortsighted bad guys, and even the more hard-core and gritty good guys are the heroes or heroines because they are making those choices for the better. And before people bring up the games where we can make all the evil choices we want, the end games of those have us make a more selfless choice to better others (even in KOTOR, we end up not being as "evil" as Malak). Those characters are also usually shown to be the noncanon version of events or a warning to not be like them as well.

ONLINE

Being online can sometimes sound like some people are assuming we're being less spiritual than them just by the way they say it. But being online in the ways we are gets us connected to people all around the world, and a surprising number of them can understand us in a way that opens the gospel to places we would never be able to go long term, but can build connections and friendships that both helps believers in those places who don't have access to as many Christian as we do, or witness to people in places we would get in trouble for doing so in normal circumstance. That way our times playing games cannot only help us grow in Christ but can also be little windows into countries where the gospel is desperately needed but is not normally permitted...all from our couches!

We may or may not be "online" all the time, but the people we come into contact with throughout our day, our month, our year, and our lifetime would certainly qualify as massive multiplayer situations (unless you work from home and don't go out very often, but you get the idea). There is a great big world we are a part of, both online and offline, full of real people for us to be involved with. We are online in the metaphorical sense here, but just like our character in real life can relate to games, our entire life relates as well, and we have a lot of influence on that experience. If you would like a great resource to share Christ with others in a less awkward way, check out the book *Share Jesus Without Fear* for a very relaxed but biblical method.

ROLE

We have to be part of a world to be in a MMORPG, and part of being in that world is our main role: evangelism. We already mentioned how it's one thing we're supposed to do even if it's not our gift, but this is more of the reason behind that call. The short answer is Jesus said to do it, so do it. But that rarely is enough to get us to go out of our comfort zone and go do something like telling people the gospel. The core of evangelism is realizing that we are Christians because someone told us about Jesus in one way or another, and that means we need to be that person for someone else because there are people who have never heard the gospel and have never heard of Jesus at all, and some of them are a lot closer than we think. Some people would be a Christian but have never had someone explain what it really means and have only had bad examples from bad video games or media that portray it wrongly. Some people just need someone to show the same love and concern that we want to be shown to us. And while we may feel that more people reject our presentation of the gospel than receive it, our job isn't to worry about if they accept it or not, our job is to honestly, sincerely, and lovingly present it and let God take care of the details.

2 Corinthians shows us how that looks in 5:18–21: "All this is from God, who through Christ reconciled us to himself and gave us the ministry of reconciliation; that is, in Christ God was reconciling the world to himself, not counting their trespasses against them and entrusting to us the message of reconciliation. Therefore, we are ambassadors for Christ, God making his appeal through us. We implore you on behalf of Christ, be reconciled to God. For our sake, he made him to be sin who knew no sin so that in him we might become the righteousness of God."

I already mentioned that concept in chapter 3, but it's worth finishing this side quest. Because Jesus went through the cross to save us, we have the much easier job of letting others know of the offer he made us. We're given the job of ambassador to appeal to others and beg (implore) them to get off the road to death. Some people get upset a good God would let so many bad things happen and let people without him go to hell, but at the same time, we do surprisingly little to solve the problems by doing our part to evangelize, tell the gospel, and give from what we've been blessed with to help with issues like poverty and starvation. Like a video game, the world won't get saved if we, a hero, just sit cutting wood rather than progress the quest. So many people get mad at God for something that's assumed to be his fault when it turned out we're the villain of the quest.

This may feel like a big job, but it starts with simply heading in the next direction we think is the right direction. Even while waiting for God to give us our next direction, we can simply walk in where we were headed last (if that direction is at all toward God). Once we have a direction we're heading in, all we have to do is pay attention and be open to God redirecting us. That way we'll always be going where God wants us to because even if he doesn't give us a different direction specifically, we'll be doing our job and heading somewhere toward him.

It isn't a random or lazy approach to life as some might see it. It's very much like a linear video game in that when we're not sure where the next part is, we can always head toward the "bad guys" or the "danger." For us in this case, that means working to win the people we see as "bad" toward God's cause and fight the real, spiritual, bad guys. Then we stay open to where he wants us to go, just like while we try to explore as much as possible, we follow the game's path when it is linear.

This is not just logical or video game based, but it was also how Paul the Apostle operated, traveling to where God called him to specifically every time, and then continuing that way until God stopped him and/or redirected him, and then when God spoke more clearly to direct him, he went right away. One instance of this is found in Acts 16:6–10 and perfectly shows my point. They were traveling to certain cities sharing the gospel, but then the Holy Spirit didn't let him go one way, so he went another until that direction was closed, then when he had a dream from God of where to go, he went right away.

PLAYING

While I use the term "playing" here, what I mean is we're the one who is in control of our lives. There may be a lot in them that we have no control over, but there is still the core aspect of ourselves that we have to decide what we will do and how we will respond to those things that we can't control. Just like with salvation, we can't control where we start, but we can control where we end, and we may not be able to control how we ended up where we are right now, but we can choose what to do from here.

We may feel at more of a disadvantage in our personal MMORPG than if Joker took over the entire building and we're in the bottom level and have to get all the way out. Some of us feel like we have more struggles in our lives than a grass Pokémon has type disadvantages (fire I get, but ice, poison, flying, AND bug, are you kidding me! And then my moves aren't good against dragon and steel also!). But wherever we are and however much feel against us, we have the ultimate ally in our struggles, the God of the universe. None of our disadvantages are a final say in him. We may still have Joker's hordes of baddies or a Bug-Fire-Ice Gym to go against, but with him at our side, we can win that fight and come out on top in the sense that we know our future is not just good but perfect in him (Revelation 21–22).

This isn't coming from someone who's had a lot of entitlement or had it easy by any means. I didn't grow up with a Christian mind-set, a lot of friends, or any money, and I still have a lot of debt from choices I didn't get input on. Even when I got saved, no one discipled me until much later, and there was a lot I had to figure out by just reading the Bible over and over and asking a lot of really dumb questions. I've had death surround me from all sides and from all distances while I was literally half a world away at times, and I've been all around the world to four continents following God. I've had people take everything I did the wrong way and took what I said the worst possible way. I've had more than my "fair share" of sins done against me but also have sinned more than my "fair share" of ways. Through it all, I've seen the truth of Romans 8:28 become more and more real in my life rather than less true: "And we know that for those who love God, all things work together for good for those who are called according to his purpose." As Christians, we love God because that's how we get into God's family in the first place, so while we sometimes forget to love God as well as we should, we don't have to fear if that part of the verse applies to us or not. We also don't have to worry about if we are called because if we are believers, that means we heard his call to salvation and accepted it (John 5:24, Revelation 3:20).

GAME

Our life is real, and we don't want to treat it like a game in the sense that things have real consequences and our choices can have a lot of repercussions to them, things we can't just hit "reload last save" to erase. But our life is a game in the sense that we are the ones in control of how we act and react like we've already talked about. We also are a lot like an Animal Crossing game according to 2 Corinthians 5:1–10. We can be courageous with our lives, even if things get tense or dangerous, because our body in this life is like a tent. We don't want to destroy our tent or treat it bad because even if we are saved, our rewards in heaven are determined by if we follow Jesus well or not, and some of us who treat our tent and this life badly will be saved but without much else than eternal life (1 Corinthians 3:10–23). When we do die in Christ though, even if eternal life is all we have, we level up from a tent to a house according to that verse. In the meantime, as Paul reminds us, we stay courageous even when life gets difficult, depressing, dangerous, disappointing, or other descriptive-of-life words that start with *d*.

Another part of our game is to not let anyone make us feel guilty for gaming as long as we are glorifying him with them. Yes, we can sometimes play them a little too long, and it's important for us as gamers to take the time to be doing the other things in life, like school or work or time with friends and family in person. And, yes, sometimes we ARE just "wasting" time with them, but that's just as valid of a way to waste time as other people's hobbies, but we still don't want to feel guilt over our games. 2 Corinthians 7:10 puts it this way, "For godly grief produces a repentance that leads to salvation without regret, whereas worldly grief produces death."

We don't want death, so we don't want worldly grief and guilt. We stay open to God and godly grief and conviction if he wants to let us know that we need to tone some game time back a little or lay off certain games for a time, but we let it be conviction rather than the worldly guilt people try to put on us. Sometimes we will have to practice our self-control with how much we play games, or we have to pause the games to do things in life that are priorities. Sometimes, we may even have seasons where gaming takes a back seat to other things in life, like work or families. But those choices are ours to make, and we have to make sure we're choosing them, rather than letting grief or guilt make us. We may need a good friend at times to tell us when we're a little too into our games, but it's not a part of us; we have to just throw out to follow God, and the quantity of time we spend needs to be something we're honestly working with God to figure out.

To Sum It All Up

At the end of the day, others may still not get our gaming, like a mom who thinks we're not sick anymore because we're playing a video game or someone who just doesn't enjoy them so they will never understand why we do so much, but we can be sure that God and those who've read this book will get it. Use the resources in the next chapter as a quick reference guide, help to grow, and reminders for the road ahead. Don't forget to note your achievements and come up with more of your own as well. And if we put all this into practice, we can be sure that there are multiple things we can do to make our time with God fully "leveled up" and, sure, that even in our video games, we are glorifying him.

I hope this book has made more sense than either of the following: (1) finding fresh food in a thousand-year-old container deep inside a sealed dungeon or (2) the weird difference between getting hurt in game (looks like I'll need half a potion) vs. getting hurt in a cut scene (and they're gone forever...okay). I hope that all this has really helped make some practical changes in your life to help you find God in your video games.

We all know it's dangerous to go alone...so take this book with you as you go!

Chapter Questions

1. Which aspect of the MMORPG stood out to you the most?
2. What are some interactions you need to be more intentional about?
3. Which way seems easier for you to evangelize, online or in person?
4. How do you feel about your life at this point of the game?
5. What are some ways you need to play differently now?

Achievement Unlocked:
IT'S BRIGHT OUT HERE

CHAPTER 13

Endgame Credits

List of Verses Used in Book

Ch. 1: Philippians 2:12, Matthew 7:21–23, Romans 10:9–13, 1 John 2:19, 2 Corinthians 13:5, John 3:16, Revelation 20:7–15, 2 Corinthians 11:14–15

Ch. 2: 2 Corinthians 6:2, Philippians 3:12–15

Ch 3: Romans 3:9–20, 23–24, Galatians 5, Revelation 20–21, 7:9, 1 John 1:7, 1 Peter 1:15, Ephesians 2:10, 2 Corinthians 5:17, 20–21, Matthew 28:18–20, 1 Corinthians 6:20, 10:31, Psalm 7:17, Psalm 30:4, 1 Thessalonians 5:18, Ephesians 5:22–23, 1:13, 4:30, Galatians 6:7–8, 1 Timothy 6:12, Jeremiah 6:16

Ch. 4: Colossians 3:8–9, 2 Timothy 3:16, James 1:22–25, Matthew 7:24–27, Colossians 3:16, Psalm 145:18, James 4:2–4, Ephesians 1:15–19, Acts 3:1–6, 6:5–6

Ch. 5: Matthew 6:16–18, Psalm 150, 1 Thessalonians 5:11, Hebrews 10:24–25, Mark 2:23–28, Acts 20:7, 1 Corinthians 16:2

Ch. 6: Acts 2:42, 1 Corinthians 1:9, Hebrews 10:24–25, Hebrews 13:16, Psalm 102:18–22, 1 Corinthians 14:26, 2 Corinthians 2:5–8, Galatians 6:1–5, Ephesians 4:11–15, Romans 2:4, Philippians 1:15–18, James 3:1, Ephesians 4:11–16, 1 Corinthians 12, Ephesians 5:25, Luke 7:36–50, 2 Corinthians 9:7, 2 Corinthians 9:6, 2 Corinthians 9:11

Ch. 7: Ezekiel 45:9, Matthew 26:51–52, Ephesians 4:31, Colossians 3:8, Matthew 21:12–13, James 1:19–20, Ephesians 4:26,

Matthew 5:28, 1 Corinthians 6, James 4:1–4, 1 John 1:8, Proverbs 24:16, 1 John 1:9, 1 John 3:6–8, Romans 12:2, James 1:21, 1 Corinthians 10:13, Hebrews 11:25, Romans 6:23, 1 John 5:16–18, 2 Corinthians 10:5, Malachi 3:5, 1 Corinthians 6:9–10, 2 Peter 2:14, Revelation 2:22, James 4:7, Romans 8:13, Proverbs 16:32, Genesis 39, Romans 2:4, Acts 19:20

Ch. 8: Luke 10:18, 2 Corinthians 2:10–11, Romans 16:20, Ephesians 6:12, 2 Corinthians 4:4, Job 1:6; 1 Chronicles 21:1; Zechariah 3:1, Acts 26:18, Revelation 20–22, 1 Peter 5:8, John 8:44, 1 Timothy 5:14, 1 Peter 5:8, Revelation 12:9, James 4:7, 1 John 3:8, Revelation 20:10, Ephesians 6:12, Romans 12:17–21, Acts 19:11–16, Galatians 5:19–21, Colossians 2:18, 1 John 4:1:3, 5:18–19, Revelation 21:8, 22:15, 1 John 4:4, Ephesians 6:10–20, John 8:44, Galatians 6:2, Ephesians 4:16, Philippians 2:4, Hebrews 11:1–3, Ephesians 2:8, Ephesians 4:14, 2 Corinthians 10:3–4, Hebrews 4:12, James 2:19, 2 Peter 2:1–4, John 10:28, 2 Timothy 2:10–13, Colossians 3:1–4, Jude 8–10, James 1:22, Hebrews 12:1

Ch. 9: Romans 1:18–20, Esther 4:16, 1 Kings 19, Matthew 17:20, Luke 16:10, John 6:1–14, John 14:6, Genesis 3, 11, Romans 1:21–25, 2 Corinthians 5:21, 1 Corinthians 10:23, 10:31, 1 Corinthians 3:12–16, Revelation 16, 21, Ephesians 4:15, 2 Corinthians 5:18–21, John 14:6, Romans 5:8, Revelation 21:6, Hebrews 12:2, John 17:14–19

Ch. 10: 1 Corinthians 12, Acts 1, 2 Timothy 4:20, Deuteronomy 13, Jeremiah 28, 1 Corinthians 14, Romans 12:3–8, Ephesians 4:11–12, Matthew 19:12, 1 Corinthians 7, Matthew 19:10–12, Galatians 5:19–21, Colossians 3:5–6, 1 Peter 4:10–11, Acts 5:41, James 1:2, 1 Peter 3:13–17, Matthew 5:11, 1 Peter 4:12–19, Revelation 12:11, Psalm 116:15, 1 Peter 4:12–19, 1 Corinthians 13:3, Philippians 1:21, Acts 4:32–37, 1 Corinthians 13:3, Matthew 19:16–30, John 14:26, Acts 9:31, Romans 8:26–27, Nehemiah 9:30, John 16:8, Ephesians 4:30, 2 Timothy 4:3–4

Ch. 11: 2 Timothy 4:5, John 3:16, Revelation 21:6, Romans 12:19, James 2:23, Revelation 2:4–5, Psalm 87:7, Psalm 149:3, Psalm

150:4, Zephaniah 3:17, Genesis 17:17, Genesis 21:6, Job 8:21, Psalm 126:2, Ecclesiastes 3:4, Luke 6:21, Job 11:14, Proverbs 28:13, Matthew 6:1–2, 1 Corinthians 11:31–32, Galatians 6:5, James 4:17, James 2:14–17, Ephesians 2:8–9, 1 John 2:1–2, Luke 10:27, Romans 14

Ch. 12: Leviticus 6:10, 1 Peter 5:7, 2 Corinthians 5:18–21, Revelation 21–22, Romans 8:28, John 5:24, Revelation 3:20, 2 Corinthians 5:1–10, 1 Corinthians 3:10–23, 2 Corinthians 7:10

Achievements from the Book

Ch. 1: **NOT A N00B:** Take your first steps to leveling up your relationship with God

Ch. 2: **AND THEY'RE OFF:** Press the start button on your relationship with God

Ch. 3: **WHO ARE YOU?:** Find out who you are in Christ

Ch. 4: **ALL BY MYSELF:** Get the basics down in Solo Mode

Ch. 5: **I THINK I SURVIVED:** Put Hardcore Mode into practice

Ch. 6: **ASKING FOR A FRIEND:** See the value of community in Christ

Ch. 7: **LOADING SAVE FILE...:** Get past sins and into freedom

Ch. 8: **DANTE WOULD BE PROUD:** Know the enemy, and how to beat him

Ch. 9: **RABBITS AND CHICKENS:** See God's Easter eggs everywhere

Ch. 10: **REDUNDANCY IS OKAY:** Unlock some achievements for Jesus

Ch. 11: **BUTTON MASHING WORKS:** Get the best mods for Jesus

Ch. 12: **IT'S BRIGHT OUT HERE:** Step outside and do something for Jesus

Some Achievement Ideas

Finish the whole Bible, beat a temptation, get a job we enjoy, find a good church, get married (if called to that), get baptized (if not yet and a believer), get a certain number of items in a collection of ours, help someone become a Christian, get a set time with God, pick a hike or marathon and complete it, start a prayer journal, see an answered prayer, just to name a few ideas.

The last page includes the achievements from this book, so cut them out and add them to your own achievements list wherever it is!

Resources

Bible Study Ideas

Youversion is a great app that has a wide variety of Bible studies, reading plans, and gives reminder notifications, so it's almost hard to miss a day

Bible in a year plans are great to keep us on track, and there are many that don't just make us read it straight through from Genesis to Revelation (called blended plans). https://www.questionsgod.com/bible-reading-plans.htm has many different kinds to find as well as the Youversion app.

Some things I like to do is to keep my Bible where I'll see it so I don't forget, even put it on something like my controller so I don't play before I've read, put my reading plan on a mirror or wall I see every day to remember, and, of course, there's my audio Bible while playing video games.

We can also learn more about the persecuted church in history and in the world today by visiting the Voice of the Martyrs at persecution.com

Spiritual Gifts Tests

These are some online gift tests. They aren't hard to find but try a variety of them and see if they fit, then try using the gifts.

Team Ministry: https://gifts.churchgrowth.org/spiritual-gifts-survey/
Spiritual Gift Test: https://spiritualgiftstest.com/
Rock Church: https://www.sdrock.com/giftstest/
Lifeway: https://www.lifeway.com/en/articles/women-leadership-spiritual-gifts-growth-service

Video Games Referenced

Please, do not assume that because I reference a game, I am endorsing it as a game you should play. Many of my games where played before I was a Christian or before I had discernment and are included for the reference itself for some gamers who have played the same game. Please, look at the ratings of each game and the content before playing it, especially if the rating is above your age recommendation. Use wisdom, ask others because there's a lot you cannot unsee in some games. I've listed them by rating for easier filtering.

Rated E (Everyone): Pokémon, Super Mario, Pong, F-Zero, Animal Crossing, Sonic the Hedgehog, NBA 2K20, Earthworm Jim 3D, Mario Kart, Gran Turismo, F1 2019, Wolverine: Adamantium Rage

Rated E+10 (Everyone 10 and up): Lion King, Legend of Zelda (Breath of the Wild as an example), Contra, Kingdom Hearts, Portal, Minecraft, Myst, Rime, StarFox Zero, Harvest Moon, The Secret of Monkey Island, Super Smash Brothers: Ultimate (Melee and Brawl are teen), Undertale

Rated T (Teen): Final Fantasy, Age of Empires II, F-Zero GX, Dynasty Warriors, Guitar Hero (a few are E+10), Star Wars: Knights of the Old Republic, Overwatch, Fortnite, World of Warcraft, Batman: Arkham Asylum/City, Shadow of the Colossus, Baldur's Gate, Star Wars: Battlefront, Dead Cells

Rated M+17 (Mature, 17 and up): Half-Life, Skyrim, God of War, Assassin's Creed, Dead Space, StarCraft, Metal Gear (almost all games), Silent Hill, Halo, Call of Duty, Morrowind, Dante's Inferno, Bioshock, Elder Scrolls Online, Dark Souls, Resident Evil, Dishonored, Mass Effect, Borderlands, Fable, Oblivion, Far Cry, Devil May Cry, Titanfall, Mortal Kombat, Doom (all titles), Ghost of Tsushima

No rating: The Stanley Parable

Personal Favorite Video Games

Here are some of my personal favorite games, not all of them are endorsements as a whole or of every single game in the series, but in general the ones I enjoyed the plot, game play, or characters of. As some of them were before I was saved or knew the lessons from this book, please, always check the ratings and content before choosing to play them yourself:

The Legend of Zelda series, the Elder Scrolls series, the Fallout series, the Dynasty / Samurai Warriors series, Portal 1 and 2, the Batman Arkham series, Animal Crossing, the Mega Man series, Pokémon, the Final Fantasy / Kingdom Hearts series, the Knights of the Old Republic series, Dishonored, Halo, and the Bioshock series.

Special Thanks To:

Jesus, because none of it matters without him

My family because their love and support have made all the difference

My sister, Juliarose, for making the awesome cover art and Beta reading

My friends, who have played countless hours with me or watched me play.

Mentors who helped me with my spiritual growth enough to be able to write a book like them and who helped me polish and think through the book itself

My publisher because you're holding this book because of them, and I really appreciate them making a life's dream of mine come true

Video games for the stories, the help, the inspiration, and more!

Bonus Achievement Unlocked:

"PARTING IS SUCH SWEET SORROW": Find God in your video games and level up your time with him

Take your achievements with you!

NOT A N00B: Take your first steps to leveling up your relationship with God	**AND THEY'RE OFF:** Press the start button on your relationship with God	**WHO ARE YOU?:** Find out who you are in Christ
ALL BY MYSELF: Get the basics down in Solo Mode	**I THINK I SURVIVED:** Put Hardcore Mode into practice	**ASKING FOR A FRIEND:** See the value of community in Christ
LOADING SAVE FILE…: Get past sins and into freedom	**DANTE WOULD BE PROUD:** Know the enemy and how to beat him	**RABBITS AND CHICKENS:** See God's Easter Eggs everywhere
REDUNDANCY IS OKAY: Unlock some achievements for Jesus	**BUTTON MASHING WORKS:** Get the best mods for Jesus	**IT'S BRIGHT OUT HERE:** Step outside and do something for Jesus
"PARTING IS SUCH SWEET SORROW": Find God in your video games and level up your time with him		

About the Author

Patrick loves the Bible, video games from all systems, history, reading, and being out in nature. He loves taking hard-to-understand ideas and making them more simple and helping others understand.

He is a Tampa, Florida, native living in Floyd, Virginia, with his wife and children. He has been all around the world doing all sorts of adventures, from being a missionary in Thailand; to a history teacher in Riner, Virginia—following God wherever He calls, to four continents so far.

Find him on

Instagram: levelupyourtimewithgod
Facebook: Level up your time with God
Twitter: @luytwg

CPSIA information can be obtained
at www.ICGtesting.com
Printed in the USA
BVHW051111260421
605873BV00019B/2362

9 781098 083960